THE PENGUIN CLASSICS

FOUNDER EDITOR (1944–64): E. V. RIEU

EDITORS:

ROBERT BALDICK (1964–72)
BETTY RADICE

BRIAN STONE wrote his first book, *Prisoner From Alamein* (1944), as a very young man. After the war, during which he was decorated, he entered the teaching profession and taught English in boys' schools for eleven years. He then trained teachers for ten years at Loughborough and Brighton, and he is now Reader in Literature at the Open University. He has two other translations to his credit in the Penguin Classics: modern English renderings of *Sir Gawain and the Green Knight* and *The Owl and the Nightingale, Cleanness* and *St Erkenwald*. He is married and has four sons and a daughter.

Medieval English Verse

TRANSLATED
WITH AN INTRODUCTION BY
BRIAN STONE

*

What can a swan need but a swan?
W. B. YEATS: *Calvary*

PENGUIN BOOKS

Penguin Books Ltd, Harmondsworth, Middlesex, England
Penguin Books Inc., 7110 Ambassador Road, Baltimore, Maryland 21207, U.S.A.
Penguin Books Australia Ltd, Ringwood, Victoria, Australia

—

First published 1964
Reprinted 1966, 1968, 1970
Reprinted with revisions 1971
Reprinted 1973

—

—

Made and printed in Great Britain
by Cox & Wyman Ltd,
London, Reading and Fakenham
Set in Monotype Fournier

Contents

Foreword

This book is an anthology, in translation, of English poetry of the thirteenth and fourteenth centuries. Short poems, made up of religious and secular lyrics, moral, political, polemical, and comic verse, account for about half the contents, and the rest is composed of short narrative poems, the longest of which is 'Pearl' (1,212 lines). The choice of poems was directed by the desire to give the general reader an idea of the scope of shorter poems in Middle English; except that, there being so few love lyrics, all which did not defy translation were included. The poems are grouped by subject, and identified chiefly by first lines, many of the titles suggested by editors having been jettisoned. These principles of selection and arrangement made possible a series of introductory essays which, taken with the main Introduction, are meant to give, besides information and critical comment for the understanding and appreciation of the poems, a view of the age as the background to its poetry.

The translator, confronting the poetry of a remote place or time, knows that he must produce a 'true' equivalent for his original: to revert to the bird image in the superscription to this book, he must find a mate for the swan of the original poem. Yet he discovers that the language of his originals colours the thought as well as shaping it; that the requirements of stanza form, rhyme, and alliteration not only shape the thought, but direct its expression and dictate its vocabulary, both that of plain meaning and that of imagery. And this applies equally to the language of the translator. So some translators use free verse, or prose, replacing the music of the original with a different music, or with none at all. Their virtue is that they give the plain meaning – if a poem may be said to have a content which is separable from its form. But the result will be a work of taxidermy, not the creation of a living swan. Indeed, some regard all verse translators as taxidermists: we ought to be a humble breed, striving at whatever cost not to produce stuffed ducks.

If one were to isolate the content of medieval English lyric poetry, one would find that its narrow range of ideas and its simplicity of feeling made it exist not so much as individual expression, but as generally held notions in heavily adorned and, above all, musical forms. The abandonment of these forms appears to be worse taxidermy than occasional infidelity to thought or image: the greater the adornment and musical quality of a poem, the more important it becomes to reproduce the original form in translation. With this principle as guide, it seemed likelier that the translator would have the experience of Miss Iris Murdoch's James Donaghue: 'It's like opening one's mouth and hearing someone else's voice emerge.' Most of these translations, then, follow the metres of their originals, and where significant departures occur, acknowledgement is made.

In entering this world of medieval prosody, the reader whose ear is attuned to the largely iambic tyranny which sat on our poetry for half a millennium until recent times should be prepared to relax into the freedom of accentual verse without notice, and not only in 'Pearl' and 'Patience'. It is a time of transition, and Romance prosody has not quite won the field.

With regard to language, the revival of ancient modes of thought, feeling, and action necessarily involves archaism, if the truth of the originals is to be evoked at all. What the translator must do is avoid, as far as possible, the clichés of archaism associated with nineteenth-century romantic writing, because they are empty and discredited. This is especially difficult when translating religious lyrics, because the imagery of devotional writing has changed little in the last seven hundred years, and because the stanza forms and rhyme schemes found in modern hymnals are similar to, and merely simpler than, those used in the thirteenth and fourteenth centuries. Ours is 'an age which has hardly produced a hymn which can be sung without embarrassment' (Miss Helen Gardner, in *The Art of T. S. Eliot*). And in the translation of love poetry, it must be remembered that stock medieval imagery lost its value as poetic currency at least as long ago as Shakespeare's 'My mistress' eyes are nothing like the sun'.

On the whole, the narrative and polemical modes, with their greater freedom and particularity, should give the translator his best opportunity and the reader most pleasure, although their metrical requirements are often no less stringent. The Middle Ages is one of the great periods of the lost art of narrative poetry: the fourteenth century produced Chaucer, Langland, Gower (all of whom are represented in translation elsewhere in this series), and the poet of *Sir Gawain and the Green Knight*, two of whose four poems are translated here. But besides being the best medium for writers of genius, narrative poetry, in a society largely subsisting on an oral tradition, often meant no more than story set up in rhyme and rhythm for declaiming or chanting. It was an accepted critical dictum of the time that, if something was well expressed in prose, it must be better expressed in verse. Narrative poetry thus fulfilled a wide function of entertainment. The elegiac spirituality of 'Pearl', the idealistic romancing of 'Sir Orfeo', and the rollicking bawdry of 'Dame Siriz and the Weeping Bitch' stretched the persona of this single translator in very different ways.

I should like to acknowledge my absolute dependence on the editors whose published texts of the original poems form the basis of this book: the Appendix, 'Provenance of the Poems', gives full details. I wish to thank Father Morson, O.C.R., of Mount Saint Bernard Abbey, Leicestershire, for material used in the commentary on poems nos. 3 and 4, and for the translation of the Latin parts of those poems; and to express my gratitude to the several friends whose criticism of work in progress has helped me, whether I have taken their advice or not.

B.E.S.

Loughborough and Brighton Training Colleges
1960–3

Introduction

An uncut umbilical cord holds every man to the society which gave him birth. It even holds the poet, for all that his being gives him visionary and aesthetic powers above those of other men; and it held the medieval poet especially. He lived in an age when poetry was transmitted orally, and when there was no question of his making a living by writing for a select but scattered audience. He was under a special disability in that printing had not been invented, and it was only towards the end of the period that the skill of handwriting was at all widely exercised. Like the masons who built and adorned the churches, and the musicians who shared with him in making pious utterance for cloister, or fantasy and frolic for castle hall or market place, the poet had to serve his immediate community. The social nexus held all tightly: the feudal way of life, with its hard laws and rigid stratifications, and the Church, with its authority over moral and intellectual life, were twin Leviathans in the sea of the artistic consciousness. In an age which knew no copyright, castle or church patronage alone could make the poet's life secure; otherwise, he must dare the minstrel fellowship of the road, and promiscuously woo baron or priest as he encountered them.

It seems right, therefore, to give a brief panoramic description of the age, and then to allow the poems, or groups of poems, with their specific introductions, to express the detail. If to the ideas embodied in 'Castle' and 'Church', the reader can add knowledge of what, on the evidence, the daily and imaginative life of the people appears to have been, of what Celtic left in medieval England, and Provençal brought to it, and of what the Norse experience meant in retrospect, he will be better able to see into the life behind the poems, and so to enjoy them.

To take the last first: the Norman Conquest (a Norse matter, because the Normans were 'Northmen' who had conquered northern France, become in some social and linguistic matters almost French, and had then launched across the Channel before being assimilated by the southerly ethos) was crucial for the development of the

PENGUIN BOOKS INC
72 FIFTH AVENUE
NEW YORK, NEW YORK 10011
ATT: COLLEGE DEPARTMENT

EXAMINATION COPY QUESTIONNAIRE

Here is an examination copy of a Penguin book FOR COURSE ADOPTION CONSIDERATION. We shall greatly appreciate receiving from you the following information. Thank you for your cooperation.

Book Title:_____

Course Description:_____

_____ Is the level of this book appropriate for your students?
       Too elementary?_____Too advanced?_____

_____As a text, this book will serve well as
       Basic____Supplementary____Suggested Reading____

_____I am planning to use this book and will be ordering approximately_____copies.*

_____I am not planning to use this book because_____

_____

For any additional comments or criticisms please use the space below or write directly to Penguin Books (see reverse side).

Name_____ Position _____

School Address_____

_____ Zip_____

*Advance information on the probable size of an order is very helpful to a publisher in estimating stock requirements.

English language. Previous invaders of England had been Germanic, speaking languages which enriched the native vocabulary while beginning the process of undermining the system of inflexions upon which Anglo-Saxon was based. But Norman French was a language of a quite different kind, and although eventually it enriched English with a vast Romance vocabulary and range of synonyms, its first effect, being the language of the conquerors and so of government generally, was to accelerate the decline of Old English. The Anglo-Saxon Chronicle lingered on for a century after the Conquest, and when the first subsequent major English poem, *The Owl and the Nightingale*, appeared at the very end of the twelfth century, the language was recognizably English of the Middle Ages, in which native and French elements jostled rather than mingled. It was not until after Chaucer's time that a native English speaker sat on the throne. For two hundred years after the Conquest, literary communication in English had been mainly in the hands of the Church, which filtered its Latin wisdom through the vernacular to its flock, and the minstrels, pragmatic versifiers, many of whom must have been multi- or bi-lingual. Latin is the dominant language in literature surviving from the thirteenth and fourteenth centuries: Anglo-Norman decreasingly, and English increasingly, make up the balance. The English content is mostly poetry, sermon and prayer, often in combination, and it is with these three that written English in the language which was to develop into ours began. The emergence of known poets, writing for a cultured society – Chaucer, Langland, Gower – came only towards the end of the period.

A characterization of feudalism shows it as the force of temporal law, the determinant of land ownership, occupation, and class, the notion of earthly order. It prescribed the duties of man and woman, and its despotic orderliness was seriously challenged only towards the end of the period, when the Black Death (1348) had so reduced the working population that survivors found bargaining power in the scarcity of their labour, and when developing trade, harbinger of the Renaissance, created a mercantile class which came in its rise to depend less and less upon barons and priests. The castle was the seat of a power which settled the relationship between man and man, told men when and how to fight, where and when to till, where to live and whom to marry, and fought its sometimes uneasy ally, the Church, for its rights to tax and to give judgement. Its inflexible class system spread over all Western Christendom an exclusive brotherhood of chivalry, whose chief occupation was fighting. In its battles, captured nobles conventionally were ransomed, while common soldiers and unranked civilians might be massacred. To the estate of man which the castle conceived, woman had little legal title: she was a chattel, who might be married for her wealth or connexions. She was subject to man, who might beat her provided he did not kill her, divorce her if the alliance became inconvenient (usually on grounds of consanguinity, which could be trumped up with little difficulty), and, if she were peasant and he noble, rape her at peril of merely formal retribution. Yet, as will be seen later, her role in medieval artistic life belied her legal inferiority.

But the castle was also the place of culture. Only there, outside the cloister, did wealth and privilege provide the leisure without which the arts can hardly flourish. Although a noble whose interests were hawking and soldiering was not obliged to learn to read, or to listen to any lay other than one about heroic wars, learning could penetrate his home, and almost certainly a churchman would be its chief purveyor. Indeed, this learned man's way of life beckoned to men of spirit who found themselves without land heritage. Better to influence men's minds through spiritual power, or to exercise in administration the literacy conferred by Church training, than to languish at home as a younger son. And for dowerless daughters, the same remedy could be used.

To this Church we must now turn; not to judge it, or to give an account of its activities and organization, but to see how its bearing on medieval life might have affected the matter and making of poetry, with which we are concerned. Firstly, it was the centre of learning, and provided a focus for all knowledge. Its approach was fundamentally incurious, and was dictated by deference to authority, whether ancient, as Aristotle and the Bible, or modern, as the Saints and Rome itself. Thus Albertus Magnus, writing out of the new spirit of observation which he, Roger Bacon, and others began to show in the thirteenth century, feels bound to apologize for the originality of his comments on animal and plant life.

Secondly, the Church's asceticism, backed by its authority, sought to confine the field of art. Saint Francis, with his sense of beauty and love of nature, is by no means typical: scholasticism distrusted the enjoyment of the senses, even when directed to such ends as seeing and smelling flowers, and regarded romances, drama, song, and dance as sinful. It consigned minstrels to hell, repeatedly proclaimed the depravity of dancing, and even objected sometimes to religious plays. Yet the evidence of its poetry and music, and of the architecture and decoration of its cathedrals, shows that the medieval Church well understood the principles and functions of art. It merely wanted them always to serve God.

Thirdly, the Church weighed on man with its domination: as tithe-collector and justicer, it reinforced the secular arm in levying toll on man's wealth, in punishing his moral shortcomings and above all in extinguishing his heresies. The rapid triumph of Christianity in the West had been followed by a period of consolidation and expansion in the field of thought, especially when the year 1000 passed without the world coming to an end. But with the new confidence, as the external pagan threat declined, so heresy within the Church increased, and by the end of the thirteenth century, seventy years of the Inquisition in Europe, following the military suppression of the Albigensians, had driven underground all organized unorthodoxies of faith. Humanity paid for its fourteenth-century theological calm not only with the blood of heretical martyrs, but with submission to a narrower and on the whole less spiritual discipline than before, one in which obedience to authority was paramount. (I take the characteristics of the great twelfth- and thirteenth-century heresies, the Albigensian and the Waldensian, to have been emphasis on purity of life and strict adherence to the teaching of the Gospels: these were the first Protestant sects, and to them many of the sixteenth- and seventeenth-century opponents of Rome acknowledged their indebtedness.) But significant English writing on religion has often busied itself with works more than with faith, and in the fourteenth century the Latin prose fulminations of Abbot Bromyard against vice are echoed in English poetry by Langland. All the same, the hope of heaven inspires *Piers Plowman* just as powerfully as it does the more esoteric 'Pearl'.

It is this hope of heaven that shows medieval sacred poetry at its sweetest, and if there is one poem which expresses religious sweetness more than others, and is at the same time typical of its age in outlook, it is surely the 'Love-Song of Friar Thomas de Hales' (poem no. 21). It was written before 1272 by a Franciscan who used the arts of secular poetry to recommend the heavenly spouse, that is, Christ, to a girl novice. She and her spiritual adviser are shown at the outset as the Lady of a Romance court and her minstrel might be shown, with her asking him to write a love-poem. But at once comes an eloquent denunciation of earthly love. Its transience and the mortality of its heroes and heroines are knelled at length in a manner which was to remain conventional in poetry for at least four hundred years; then, in contrast, the permanence and preciousness of the love of Christ are set forth. The last section is an exhortation to chastity, the maintenance of which, Friar Thomas says, will qualify the girl for the bliss of paradise. Direct but delicate, his poem is true to the courtly manner, as well as to the religious spirit of the age, which he expresses with charming naïveté.

Friar Thomas's poem is one of many which makes longing for the peace of the cloister credible, even attractive, and it seems that lay people, from the highest to the lowest, could feel themselves drawn to it. For within the Church, a man knew how he should live: he had status and security, and although it is clear that at least the lower orders led an arduous life, a man of learning, especially if he were of good birth, could obtain ease and comfort enough for study and writing.

The routine which held churchmen also beckoned to the laity. At the centre of every populated place stood the church; big enough to hold most of the inhabitants, for church attendance was compulsory, although, then as now, more women than men seem to have attended. As Gregory the Great had shrewdly recognized hundreds of years before, when decreeing that pagan temples should not be pulled down, but converted to Christian use, the place of worship was the habitual and natural place of resort for members of the community. There they gathered for solemn and joyous celebrations of the Christian calendar, for the feasts of the different seasons, and for special occasions of disaster or rejoicing. Church provided the only regular meeting-place for residents of scattered localities who would be free from toil, by strict injunction, only on the church-going day: it is not surprising that there was no tradition of silence during worship, and that officiating priests often had to quell general conversation. The service was conducted amid distractions unknown to our days: it seems to have been necessary to warn people against presumptuous behaviour and dress in church, and against contact with undesirable characters, especially seducers, in the crowd. There are also references to kings and nobles carrying on the administration of government during the Mass itself, and to knights scratching pictures of tournament life on stone-work during sermons. As the biggest and most permanent building in the neighbourhood, the church might on occasion have to do duty as a grain store, or as a fortified place. These details are not given in order to denigrate the power and sanctity of the medieval church – although the age has been described as one of acquiescence rather than of faith[1] – but to indicate the complete acceptance of the Church and all that it stood for, in daily life, and so in literature. In the romances, mention is repeatedly made of the characters of chivalry at worship; and at the other end of the gamut, church people and situations provide the basis for many low and comic songs.

Thus Castle and Church prescribed the whole way of life: they could not conceive of individual rights existing outside their systems, and so did not recognize or tolerate any kind of non-conformism. Their impulse was what we now call totalitarian, and they aimed to establish complete control of man's political and religious thoughts, as well as his actions. Most of their judges were prosecutors and juries as well. Fortunately, medieval totalitarians did not possess the equipment for enforcement which dictators have today, and their system was gradually to loosen, under the pressure of such events as the Peasants' Revolt of 1381, and the increasing centralization of temporal government by ever stronger kings, who in their own interest limited local autonomy of baron and priest. The mass of poetry produced under the direct stimulus of the Church thus tended to reflect common assumptions and dogmas, and that on political subjects to follow strictly contemporary partisanships, as one would expect of a time of warring faction.

Undisputed though these two major powers might be, particularly in the life of public expression, and hence in art, civilization was so rudimentary that they might appear as little more than rocks in the main stream of ordinary life. The struggle to wring subsistence from beast and crop, to survive pestilence, famine, and war, made for an extraordinarily hard and perilous life, which disrupted families on a scale unknown today, and forced every small group to rely on its own resources. Since society could take care of people to a very limited

1. By Professor G. G. Coulton in *Medieval Panorama*, page 458.

extent, its two main powers could attract allegiance only after the powers of nature had been satisfied. These were vividly personified by the superstitious temper of the age. Christianity provided only a sublimated seasonal ritual, and the force of the old dispensation thus remained in men's, and particularly women's, minds. The absolutism of the Church tended to allot to the Devil all that had not been formally blessed into its fold – heathens, the whole of brute and plant creation, unbaptized infants, and all unexplained phenomena whatever; diseases of the body and mind, drought, tempest, blight. All these were under the control of pagan gods, or devils, as the Church called them; and scepticism as to the existence of these supernatural beings was rarely expressed, either inside or outside the Church. Moreover, concentration on the miraculous in religion, which, contrary to New Testament teaching, was used to spread and consolidate the faith, positively encouraged superstition.

So pagan rituals and magical practices of all kinds flourished, sometimes dressed in Christian style, sometimes not. Since the old religion offered more practical things to do, in the way of charms, spells, and ceremonies in the daily and annual rounds, it was evidently felt as supplementary to the new one which anathematized it. Very broadly speaking, it recommended identity with nature instead of withdrawal from it, fertility instead of chastity, amoral acceptance of all life's offerings rather than purposeful selection from them. Women, who had such an insignificant place in the formal organization of the new society, guarded the lore and formulae of the old at their hearths, often led its dances and other ceremonies, and so became the main quarry in the witch-hunts which disfigured Christian Europe for six hundred years. Their spirit, on the whole a peaceful, passive, suffering spirit of love, which could vary its homely piety with ecstasy, suffuses the popular literature of the Middle Ages, and even softens the rigidity of masculine militancy in religious writing. Within Christianity, women's natural devoutness adapted itself to the new dignity of holy chastity, and the treatises and poems written for (and perhaps sometimes by) these women sound a tender note which makes a seemly contrast to the coarse or tragic stridency often evoked in literature by the lot of woman in the world outside. And it is the feminine half of human genius that produced the most original characteristic of the Middle Ages, one which has affected nearly all subsequent love-poetry, and largely moulded the polite conventions governing relations between the sexes ever since that time.

This was courtly love. But before we consider it, we must mention the remains in England of Celtic culture, and particularly those which affected literature. Waves of vigorous barbarians from the east had driven the Celts westward, but, just as the Irish kind of Christianity had taken each wave in turn and done something to civilize it, so the Arthurian legends had withstood the invaders. Indeed, the Anglo-Saxon immigrants and their Norse successors had their own traditions of romancing about the past, and the strong spirit which had infused epic and saga took kindly to the legendary materials of the conquered native races. When the Church had to surrender its last tittle of independence to Rome, and the body politic became French-speaking, the heroic tales of Arthur and his knights gained fresh currency in the new languages. Geoffrey of Monmouth, the first to write down the whole Arthurian cycle, and its presenter to Europe early in the twelfth century, gave England a noble past and a rival to the French Charlemagne, and when the courtly civilization of Provence arose, its epitome of chivalry was the shadowy Arthur, not the all-too-historical, canonized, Charlemagne.

The blend of the old Celtic stories – their visionary fury of passion, battle, and myth set in a cool, green land defies brief characterization – with the Provençal ideas of chivalry and courtly love, gave form to Romance and a basis to medieval secular literature all over Europe.

The foundation of the spirit of courtly love is the belief that woman is a lofty creature to whom service is due, and who ennobles the man whose love she possesses, whether she rewards him with her love or not. The lover's service must be total, as that of vassal to lord: his lady, like the lord in the alternative social system, and God in the alternative religion, is perfect and must not be adversely criticized.

The origin of these extraordinary ideas is not known. Speculation can merely glance at the passions and ideas informing previous love-poetry, and then guess at the synthesis which sparked into being, at about the beginning of the twelfth century, the courtly love-lyric. The Moors may have been partly responsible; Arabic and Hebrew love-songs, to which were added Spanish refrains, appear to have brought a new feeling to Europe – a glittering Mozarabic passion.

Then there are the Latin love-poems of the Dark Ages, sensual and often tender; and every Latin scholar knew Ovid, who made rules in poetry for the conduct of scandalous love. Of course the religion of love described in *Ars Amatoria* is a sham religion, but the poet concentrates on the means and modes of gratifying sexual passion, which is a kind of exaltation of it. Exaltation, however, is the last treatment accorded to sexual passion in classical or early medieval literature. It was a passion which could produce tragic aberration, if a highly placed person, like Dido, accorded it undue importance, but on the whole the treatment of it fits into the ancient pattern of honour (Tarquin and Lucrece, Appius and Virginia). Whatever other influences there may have been on the development of medieval love-poetry, the long unbroken tradition of Latinity must be chief: Latin was the main vehicle of culture, and only civilized and leisured people could find time to cultivate such an 'art of love' as courtly love. Where life is lived on subsistence level, man has no motive for elevating to a pedestal one who fulfils necessities of his bed, board, and field labour, however close his soul to hers. It was a poor Paris minstrel who said, 'Love is only for the rich!'

Since Vikings raided the Mediterranean, we have to consider the possibility of a Northern European influence on the development of courtly love. Woman had her place in those societies: sex and marital love figure in the narrative poetry, and there are even fine poems of lyrical passion, such as the Anglo-Saxon 'The Wife's Lament' and 'The Husband's Message'. But the arts are mainly concerned with man's quests in war, government and religion, not in love. Of some interest to us, however, is the appearance in Norse and Icelandic saga from time to time of a peculiar female character; a woman on fire to dominate through her menfolk, one who drives men to actions invariably brave, usually rash, and almost always tragic in consequence. These *femmes fatales* at least imposed service through passion, and their type may have contributed something to the idea of courtly love.

Then there are the ballads. If they have the ancient ancestry which is generally assumed, those apparently free from courtly influence present love as a passion between equals, in which the biologically more vulnerable is likely to suffer more. Elsewhere, woman is legitimate prey, or a subject for ribald comment, or the provider of domestic comfort. A fair statement of man's expectation of her is quoted by Eileen Power in 'Medieval People': a fifteenth-century Frenchman, an old husband of a young wife, gives her this advice on her next marriage: 'Be careful that in winter he (your husband) has good fire without smoke, and let him rest well between your breasts, and thus bewitch him.'

To turn from these diverse notions of the love relationship to medieval Christian ideas on the subject is to confront a system opposite in drift to courtly love, one which, by its very denial of all that the new erotic religion stood for, may have given strength to it. Christianity reviled the flesh: courtly love 'sanctifies the flesh by making it serve an impeccable ideal of humility and self-sacrifice, and ... heals the quarrel between the body and the soul'.[1] Aquinas saw evil in the sexual act, in so far as it submerges the rational faculty: in courtly love, passion purifies the soul:

> A man were blest in Jesu's sight
> If he could lie with her at night,
> For he'd have heaven here. (Poem no. 86)

– a fleering irony at the expense of orthodox religion.[2] As has been indicated, medieval marriage was a social convenience, but it was also a Christian sacrament, and the teaching of the Church was that sexual intercourse was for procreation and to uphold the marriage bond. Indeed passionate love of one's wife was deprecated, and might be thought adulterous. So in courtly love, marriage was irrelevant. The Lady whom the lover served could be a virgin, or someone else's wife, or a widow. Then, in the after-life of courtly lovers, as a kind of comment on Christian chastity, women who had given their favours wisely were the elect; next below them were those who had given their love to all; and lowest were those who had refused all wooers, and who spent eternity sitting on agitated thorns. The picture of Lancelot bending the knee at Guinevere's bed, as at an altar, after an adulterous encounter with his liege lord's wife, fixes the spirit of this worship in the mind. Another picture, that of King Mark abjectly spying from a tree under which his wife Iseult is wooed by Tristram (there is a carving of this scene on a misericord in Chester Cathedral),

1. Sir Maurice Bowra: *Medieval Love-Song* (the John Coffin Memorial Lecture, 1961). Like most who write on courtly love, I am indebted to Professor C. S. Lewis (Chapter 1 of *The Allegory of Love*).

2. But perhaps not so ironical. Dionysus was a god, after all: see W. B. Yeats's play *The Resurrection*.

is a comment on the challenge which it offered to the temporal governor.

In this brief outline, to which some detail will be added in the introduction to the English poems of courtly love (pages 175–82), one other characteristic must be mentioned. Service to Love is only possible for the noble heart, and in its operation the full sanctions of feudalism apply: a peasant woman may be half-forced, but love-service to a noblewoman gains merit by the loftiness of her rank or the self-abnegation of the lover. Courtly love came to be a philosophy which helped to mould the age of chivalry, and gave the great Angevin ladies of the twelfth and thirteenth centuries a basis for temporal power and spiritual rule in a society which, as we have seen, either denied or limited them in both fields. The brilliance of life in the entourages of Eleanor of Aquitaine,[1] who was the first to hold a Court of Love, and of her daughter Marie, Countess of Champagne, marks the high point of this culture.

One of the finest of French poets was 'Marie de France', probably the Plantagenet Princess who was Abbess of Shaftesbury for a score of years before 1190. That this strange double dedication of a noble lady, to the service of both Amor and Christ, could take place at all, prepares us for the fusion of courtly and religious impulses which is so often found in medieval poetry (see poem no. 38). It also explains why the Church was so unalterably opposed to courtly love, and why, when the Albigensian and Waldensian heresies, whose most numerous supporters were women, were destroyed in crusade, the Provençal royal house, home of courtly love, also fell. Women were the special prey of the Inquisition set up in Toulouse after the final battle in 1229. Only the spirit of the defeated lingered on, to infuse both the sacred and profane poetry of an age whose secret dream was one of perfect union with God or lover.

1. Wife first to Louis VII of France, then to Henry II of England.

Poems of the Nativity

The medieval joy in faith finds its best expression in lyrics on the Nativity and on the role of the Virgin Mary. The ideas of unique birth and everlasting triumph over death combine to remove all darkness from this part of the poetic scene; so that hell is no more than a hazard which Our Lady helps us to circumvent, winter and long nights are forgotten in her magical reverdie,[1] and the Middle Ages' burning sense of sin itself is lost in ecstatic rejoicing. The primary sense of these poems is wonder at the miracle of virgin birth, at divine visitation made on a sweet girl who might have been the object of a trouvère's passion but for the higher purpose which marked her off for adoration. And so the mystical union which rendered into human form the pre-existent heavenly Christ is set, in the first poem, in the April countryside of Europe, where every girl waits for her man of men. Here the dew, which in folk poetry symbolizes virginity, is not brushed away by a wooer, or dried off the flower by the sun; but rather confirmed by the heavenly visitant who is compared with it. The union is muted to a high silence, in which wonder moves tenderly to the closing doctrinal point.[2]

Although this most famous Nativity song survives from a minstrel manuscript of the early fifteenth century, its theme, the Conception in spring, had been the subject of song much earlier. Four of its lines are in fact directly quoted from the second poem, which dates from the early thirteenth century. Spring merely touches off the poem 'Bringing us bliss now'; after the beginning, only the emotion of thanksgiving joy remains to diversify the doctrinal insistence.

Poems nos. 3 and 4 are the only macaronic poems which have been included in this collection. Macaronic poetry (a specialized term, but one generally used to describe a form of verse written in two or more languages) was common in medieval times. In such

1. Old French dance song celebrating the beauties of spring.
2. For a full discussion of the poem, and especially of the biblical references to dew and their medieval allegorical interpretation, see R. T. Davies, *Medieval English Lyrics*, pp. 14–19.

poems in England, Latin was nearly always a constituent language, and combinations of it with English, or Anglo-Norman, or both, are found. The excellence of these two poems, and the limitation of their Latin content to an almost burden-like effect, may justify their inclusion. The Latin syntax of the first is chaotic: the poet seems to have been musically concerned only to provide feminine endings to his lines, so that translation of some of them is speculative. But these devotional poems must be thought of as hymns and prayers: they both combine praise and supplication in musical measure.

The second stanza of no. 3 contains a 'roe' simile. The roe as an allegory of longing in a good sense may derive from Psalm XLII, 1 ('As the hart panteth after the water brooks, so panteth my soul after thee, O God'), but usually, in both love and religious poetry, lack of restraint is implied. Hence the pejorative sense in religious poetry, as here and in 'Pearl' (stanza 29), and the commendatory sense in poems of courtly love, where excess of feeling is *de rigueur* for the lover. However, in the Bestiary, the stag (see poem no. 45) stands for two virtues.

Poem no. 4 contains two references worthy of comment. One is the Virgin Mary's popular designation as 'Star of the Sea': a beautiful idea, but one based merely on a scribal error. The effect of it is even more brilliant, however, than the conjectured printer's error in 'Brightness falls from the (h)air' of the Elizabethan poet Nashe. 'Star of the Sea' spread through the medieval Church and to succeeding ages in the following way: The Hebrew name 'Miriam' means 'a drop of the sea', which was correctly rendered into Latin by Saint Jerome, in his *Liber Interpretationis Nominorum Hebraicorum* as '*stilla maris*'. Here the copying scribe's eye or pen made the slip to give us 'stella maris'. The error in the text of Saint Jerome has been corrected only in the latest edition (*Corpus Christianorum*, vol. 72, p. 137). Further on in the poem, in the fourth stanza, occurs the 'Ave-Eva' antithesis. The idea of Mary as a second Eve, who came to repair the errors of the first, would appear to have developed as a consequence of the reference in Romans v to Christ as the second Adam. But the force of the reverse spelling may owe something to occult mysteries. 'Roma-Amor' is one reverse spelling which contained a potent idea for the ancients, and if we remember Dr Faustus's spell, in the circle of which he included

> Jehovah's name
> Forwards and backwards anagrammatized,

it is not hard to see why there was power for Christians in the 'Ave-Eva' idea. It is found as early as the ninth century in a hymn from St Gall, and its inclusion there may point to its being already current.

Poems nos. 5 and 7 are Nativity carols, the latter of which is the earliest in English yet discovered, for it appears in a Franciscan list of sermon outlines written not later than 1350. The words of the refrain clearly convey both the manner of performance and the joy of the occasion. The Virgin's song to the Christ child (no. 6) takes an imaginative leap into the Virgin's experience: its tenderness and simplicity make appraisal almost irrelevant.

1

I sing of a Maiden,
A matchless one;
King of all Kings
She chose for her Son.
In quiet he drew
To where she was,
As the April dew
Falls on the grass.
In quiet he drew
Towards her bower,
As the April dew
Falls on the flower.
In quiet he drew
To where she lay,
As the April dew
Falls on the spray.
Both mother and maiden
Was none but she:
Well may such a lady
God's mother be.

2

Bringing us bliss now, the birds are all singing;
Branches sprout leaves and the grasses are springing.
Of one that is matchless my utterance sings,
Chosen as mother by the King of Kings.

Taintless she is and unspotted by sin,
Descended from Jesse, of kingly kin.
The Lord of mankind from her womb was born
To save us from sin, who would else be forlorn.

'Hail Mary, full of grace! And may Our Lord
Be with you!' was the angel Gabriel's word.
'The fruit of your womb, I declare, shall be blest:
You shall carry a child beneath your breast.'

This greeting and word which the angel had brought,
Mary considered and pondered in thought.
She said to the angel, 'How could such thing be?
Of knowledge of man my body is free.'

She was virgin with child and virgin before,
And still virgin yet when her Baby she bore.
Never was maiden a mother but she;
Well might she the bearer of God's Son be!

Blest be the Child, and the Mother, too, blest,
And where her Son suckled, blest the sweet breast!
Praised be the time such a child was born,
Who saved us from sin, who would else be forlorn!

3

Holy Mary, mother mild,
  Mater salutaris,   Mother of salvation
Fairest flower of any field
  Vere nuncuparis.   you are truly called
With Jesus Christ you were with child;
You drive me from my musings wild
  Potente,   powerfully
Which make me go to death, I know,
  Repente.   suddenly

My thoughts are wild like any roe,
  Luto gratulante.   rejoicing in the mire
They plunge me in the utmost woe
  Illaque favente.   fondling me
But if the Christ from me should go,
I know my heart would break in two
  Fervore.   with passion
By night and day I lose my way
  Dolore.   in sorrow

Jesu, through your power and might
   Omnia fecisti: you have made all things
The Holy Ghost in Mary alit
   Sicut voluisti.   as you willed
Since we call him Lord Almighty,
Jesu, bring my thought to Christ
   Constanter,   firmly
That it shall stay, not go astray
   Fraudanter.   false-heartedly

Jesus Christ, so high aloft,
   Digno tu scandente;   worthily have you as-
                          cended
Heaven and earth below you wrought
   Victore triumphante;   triumphing in victory
With your body mankind you bought:
His soul at any cost you sought,
   Nec dare,   nor would you give him
                          away
And gave the blood that was so good
   Tam gnare.   with full knowledge

Sweetest Lady, flower of all,
   Vere consolatrix,   truly our Comforter
Be my helper lest I fall,
   Cunctis reparatrix   you who make reparation
                          for all
Gentlest Queen of chosen sway,
Be before me night and day
   Precantis!   as I pray
Give me grace to see the face
   Infantis!   of your Child

That through your sweetest prayers I may,
   Tutrix orphanorum,   O protector of orphans
Leave this world's vexatious way,
   Solamen miserorum;   O consolation of the
                          wretched
And to you, Lady, may I take
My sins and them thereby forsake
   Volente,   willingly
And so not miss your heavenly bliss:
   Poscente.   this I ask.

4

Lady Lady, fair and bright
    Velud maris stella,   *as a star of the sea*
Brighter than the day is light,
    Parens et puella,   *Mother and Virgin*
I cry to you to look on me;
Lady, pray your Son for me,
    Tam pia,   *you so kindly*
That I may closely come to you,
    Maria!   *Mary*

In grief your counsel is the best,
    Felix fecundata;   *happy one made fruitful*
For all the weary you are rest,
    Mater honorata.   *honoured mother*
Beseech him in a gentle mood,
Who shed for all of us his blood
    In cruce,   *on the Cross*
That we may come to him at last
    In luce.   *in the light*

All this earth was lost forlorn
    Eva peccatrice,   *through Eve the sinner*
Until our Lord the Christ was born
    De te genetrice.   *from you as a mother*
But with the Ave went away   *Hail (Mary)*
The lowering night, and came the day
    Salutis.   *of salvation*
The fountain gushes forth from you
    Virtutis.   *of power*

Lady, choicest blossoming,
    Rosa sine spina,   *Rose without a thorn*
You bore us Jesu, heavenly King
    Gratia divina: *by the favour of God*
In everything you bear the prize,
Lady Queen of paradise
    Electra.   *chosen*
Gentle maiden, mother es   *you*
Effecta.   *have been made*

Well he knows he is your Son,
    Ventre quem portasti;   *whom you bore in your*
                                        womb
Your prayers to him he will not shun,
    Parvum quem lactasti.   *whom as a baby you*
                                          suckled
So kindly and so good he is
That he has brought us all to bliss
    Superni,   *of heaven*
And shut for ever the foul abyss
    Inferni.   *of hell*

5

Of a Rose, a lovely Rose,
Of a Rose is all my song.

Listen, nobles old and young,
How this rose at outset sprung;
In all this world I know of none
I so desire as that fair rose.
    Of a Rose, etc.

The angel came from heaven's tower
To honour Mary in her bower,
And said that she should bear the flower
To break the Devil's chain of woes.
    Of a Rose, etc.

In Bethlehem that flower was seen,
A lovely blossom bright of sheen.
The rose is Mary, heaven's Queen;
Out of her womb that blossom rose.
    Of a Rose, etc.

The first branch is full of might,
That sprouted on the Christmas night
When star of Bethlehem shone bright,
For far and wide its lustre shows.
    Of a Rose, etc.

The second branch sprang forth to hell,
The Devil's fearful power to quell,
And there henceforth no soul could dwell.
Blessed the coming of that rose!
    Of a Rose, etc.

To heaven sprang the third shoot,
Sweet and fair, both stem and root,
To dwell therein and bring us good:
In priestly hands it daily shows.
　　Of a Rose, etc.

Let us then with honour pray
To her who is our help and stay,
And turns us from the Devil's way.
From her that holy bloom arose.
　　Of a Rose, a lovely Rose,
　　Of a Rose is all my song.

6

Jesu, son most sweet and dear,
Mean the bed you lie on here,
　　And that afflicts me sore.
For your cradle's like a bier,
And ox and ass are with you here,
And I must weep therefore.

Jesu, sweet one, show no wrath,
For I have not the poorest cloth
　　To wrap you in its fold.
Not a rag in which to wrap
You safe or hold you on my lap;
So put your feet against my pap,
　　And shield you from the cold.

7

Let us gather hand in hand
And sing of bliss without an end:
The Devil has fled from earthly land,
And Son of God is made our friend.

A Child is born in man's abode,
And in that Child no blemish showed.
That Child is God, that Child is Man,
And in that Child our life began.
　　　Let us gather, etc.

Be blithe and merry, sinful man,
For your marriage peace began

When Christ was born.
Come to Christ, your peace is due
Because he shed his blood for you,
   Who were forlorn.
     So let us gather, etc.

Sinful man, be blithe and bold,
For heaven is both bought and sold,
   Through and through.
Come to Christ, and peace foretold:
His life he gave a hundredfold
   To succour you.
   So let us gather hand in hand
And sing of bliss without an end:
The Devil has fled from earthly land,
And Son of God is made our friend.

8[1]

As I was lying down at night
And looking on the land,
I saw a Maiden there who held
An infant by the hand.

This Maiden looked so beautiful,
Her mien so sweet and pure,
That all the anguish of my grief
She certainly could cure.

I pondered on that lovely one,
And to myself I said
That she had done some good man wrong,
Unless she were a maid.

Beside her, seated, was a man:
A serious look he wore;
His speech was grave and sober and
He knew the ancient law.

The lustre waned upon his face,
And greying was his head.
He kindly asked me to remain
On hearing what I said.

'No wonder that you start,' said he,
'At what you now behold,

     1. The original is rhymed abab.

For so, indeed, did I myself,
Until the truth was told.

'How could a woman be at once
A mother and maiden pure,
And bring to birth a child without
A man defiling her?

'Unworthy though I know myself,
She is Mary, and my wife.
God knows, I never gave her child:
I love her as my life.

'I had no knowledge of her, yet
Her womb began to swell.
I truly swear it happened so,
But how, I cannot tell.

'She would not do a deed of wrong;
I trust her purity.
I know and swear that this is so,
And found it so to be.

'More likely is it that she would
Without a man conceive,
Than that she would gravely sin,
And Joseph so deceive.

'This infant lying in poverty,
In ragged wrappings pent,
Uncomfortably, meanly bound –
From heaven he is sent.

'His father is the King of Heaven,
(For so said Gabriel)
With whom this Child has equal rank,
O Emanuel!'

And so this Child that then I saw
Is, as Joseph said
And I aver, both God and man:
His Mother is a maid.

Let us worship then this Child
Both by day and night,
That we may look upon his face
In uttermost delight!

Poems on the Passion

'By moche more it is lausom (praiseworthy) to ous to have the ymage of Crist in the cros, that we in havynge mynde on the deth of Crist mowe (may) overcome the temptaciouns and the venym of the fende (Devil), the olde serpent',[1] writes an unknown fourteenth-century divine in his sermon justifying images; and by his betokening we can understand why so many poems on the Crucifixion were written. Quite simply, meditation on the central fact of his religion was the best act of faith and work an ordinary Christian could perform. His concentration helped him to understand the divine purpose and to avoid sin. Poems nos. 11, 13, 14, and 15 all derive ultimately from meditations ascribed to St Augustine, many slightly differing metrical versions of which were composed in English during the medieval period. One aspect of these poems is the 'Candet nudatum pectus' (his naked breast shines white), and another is the 'Respice in faciem Christi' (look upon the face of Christ). The dialogue poem no. 16, like the magnificent but more courtly Harley lyric on the same subject (no. 80), joins these themes with the suffering of the Mother of Christ. Possibly, as Carleton Brown suggests, the first section of the dialogue should be assigned to St John.

In these poems, the body is human in its pathos, but the precious suffering manifests itself through divine symbols which become magnified in the meditating mind until the blood of Christ fills the universe. Nails, wounds, white flesh, scourged back, pricking thorns, arms forcibly stretched, agglomerate with Gothic poignancy to the image of the crucified Christ. Him the poets see as painters and especially sculptors saw him (line 9 of no. 13 shows us the poet thinking in terms of marble), and he becomes the referent statue of all meaning, the focus of all compassion. The passage in Sir Kenneth Clark's *The Nude* (pages 221–7) on medieval and Renaissance treatment of the Crucifixion in art marvellously illuminates these poems.

1. Quoted by G. R. Owst, *Literature and Pulpit in Medieval England*, p. 141.

Poem no. 12, which is perhaps the most lyrical of the fourteenth-century religious carols, renders into musical form an important theme of meditation, the Tears of Christ. Consciousness of human unworthiness and grief for the Passion are nicely harmonized into the closing reference to the triumph of Christ. No. 10, an English insertion in St Edmund of Potigny's 'Le Merure de Seinte Eglise', which was probably written just before his death in 1240, catches in a single quatrain the graphic and emotional essentials of the Crucifixion scene.

Poem no. 17 is a versification of the Reproaches of Christ, the Latin form of which was sung as part of the Good Friday service: it was written down or composed by Friar William Herebert, a Franciscan who died at Hereford in 1333. So inescapable a reference to Jews warrants a brief account of their position in medieval England: by the time this poem was written, their political and religious anathematization was complete. William the Conqueror had brought Jews from Rouen to finance his operations, and for a hundred years they had prospered under royal protection. But nobles who owed them money, and resented their function as kings' supporters, stirred up feeling against them which, augmenting the blood-lust and fanaticism of the crusading spirit, caused the pogroms associated with the coronation of Richard Lionheart (1189) and the massacres at York, Lynn, and Stamford. In 1198 Innocent III warned kings to abandon usury, which was in any case forbidden to Christians, and a century of political and religious persecution, operating on the one hand by confiscation of wealth and property, and on the other by the closing of synagogues and execution on trumped-up religious charges,[1] ended with Honorius IV ordering his archbishops in York and Canterbury to stop all association between Christians and Jews. The banishment of Jews in 1290 saw about 16,000 destitute people sailing southwards across the Channel: until Cromwell permitted a return in 1655, there was no official Jewish community in England. So readers will not be surprised to find unpleasant anti-Jewish sentiments expressed in more than one poem in this book. To exclude these references would be desirable

---

1. Many readers will know Chaucer's Prioress's Tale, the hero of which is a Christian child murdered by Jews; and the reference in it to Hugh of Lincoln, a child imagined to have been ritually murdered in 1255. Hugh was the subject of a miracle play of 1316 and of a ballad.

but that it would be unhistorical: for medieval Christian writers, Synagogue was the blindfold girl with the broken staff, prominently sculpted on their cathedrals.

As an introduction to poems on the Crucifixion theme, the strange poem no. 9 is included. No definite source has been discovered for the story of Judas's sister, but the fearful example of Eve would perhaps make it easy for a tradition to develop which would largely exonerate the male sex from the great crime of Christian history. Among the medieval legends which are found about Judas, one assumes a previous life of crime, while a contrary one makes him a miracle-worker and most favoured of the disciples. Judas 'was somtyme so myghty goostely (powerful spiritually) and so grete with God that he reysed men from dethe to liff, he caste oute ffendes fro men and heled mesels (lepers)' (Myrc's 'Festial', following St John Chrysostom).[1] The rough dancing rhythm, the repetitions, and the use of dialogue throughout the poem and especially for dramatic climax, are characteristics of folk poetry, which find their way into the ballad. Indeed, this poem has been called the first English ballad.

9

Upon a Holy Thursday, up rose Our Lord,
And spoke to Judas gently, very mild his word:
'To Jerusalem, O Judas, and buy our commons there;
Thirty silver pieces in your wallet bear.
Far, far will you travel in the wide, wide street,
And someone in your family you well may meet.'
Judas met his sister, deceit behind her eye:
'Judas, you deserve to be stoned till you die,
Judas, you deserve to be stoned till you die
For believing in a prophet who is false, say I.'
'Hush, my darling sister, your heart may break in two:
If Christ my Lord should know of it, he'd be revenged on you.'
'Climb up the rock, my Judas, above where it is steep,
And quickly lay your head upon my lap and sleep.'
Judas, when he woke from his sleep, looked around,
And the thirty silver pieces were nowhere to be found.
He tore at his head until a bloody crown he had,
And the Jews of Jerusalem thought that he was mad.

1. Quoted by G. R. Owst op. cit., p. 125.

The wealthy Jew called Pilate came to see him there:
'Will you sell me Jesus, your lord, you declare?'
'I will not sell my Lord for wealth or property,
But just for thirty pieces he committed to me.'
'Will you sell your Master, Christ, for any sort of gold?'
'No, only for the coins that rightly he should hold.'
In came Our Lord as the Apostles sat at meat:
'Are you sitting down, apostles, and will you not then eat?
Are you sitting down, apostles, and will you not then eat?
I was bought and sold today instead of our meat.'
Then Judas stood and faced him: 'Is it me you mean, Lord?
I was never spoken evil of, at home or abroad.'
Then Peter stood and faced him, and said with all his might,
'Though Pilate were to come, Lord, with ten hundred knights,
Though Pilate were to come, Lord, with ten hundred knights,
Yet in spite of all, for your love would I fight.'
'Be at rest, Peter, your mind well I know;
Three times you shall deny me before the cock crow.'

10

Now sinks the sun beneath the wood
(Mary, I pity your lovely face):
Now sinks the sun beneath the Rood
(Mary, I pity your Son and you).

11

White was his naked breast,
And red with blood his side,
Blood on his lovely face,
His wounds deep and wide.

Stiff with death his arms
High spread upon the Rood:
From five places in his body
Flowed the streams of blood.

12

Lovely tear from lovely eye,
  Why do you give me woe?
Sorrowful tear from sorrowful eye,
  You break my heart in two.

You sigh so sore,
Your sorrow is more
Than mouth of man can tell.
In grief you sing,
Mankind to bring
Out of the pit of hell.
Lovely tear from lovely eye, etc.

I proud and wild,
You pure and mild
And free from craft and guile.
Your death you give,
Through which I live:
Blessed be that wile!
Lovely tear from lovely eye, etc.

Your mother saw
What pain you bore,
And cried out with a start:
You spoke relief
To soothe her grief;
Her sweet suit won your heart.
Lovely tear from lovely eye, etc.

Your heart is rent,
Your body bent
Upon the Cross's height:
But storm is hushed
And Devil crushed,
Jesu, by your might.

Lovely tear from lovely eye,
Why do you give me woe?
Sorrowful tear from sorrowful eye,
You break my heart in two.

13

You who created everything,
My sweet Father, heavenly King,
Hear me, I your son implore,
For Man this flesh and bone I bore.

Clear and bright my breast and side,
Blood on the whiteness gushing wide,
Holes in my body crucified.

Held stiff and stark my long arms rise,
And dim and dark fall on my eyes:
Like sculptured marble hang my thighs.

My feet are red with flowing blood,
Their holes washed over by the flood.
Show Man's sins mercy, Father on high!
With all my wounds to you I cry!

14

Man and woman, look on me!
How much I suffered for you, see!
Look on my back, laid bare with whips:
Look on my side, from which blood drips.
My feet and hands are nailed upon the Rood;
From pricking thorns my temples run with blood.
From side to side, from head to foot,
Turn and turn my body about,
You there shall find, all over, blood.
Five wounds I suffered for you: see!
So turn your heart, your heart, to me.

15

Look on your Lord, Man, hanging on the Rood,
And weep, if you can weep, tears all of blood.
For see how his head is hurt with thorn,
His face and spear-wound spat on in scorn.
Pale grows his fair cheek, and darker his sight,
Now droops on the Cross his body bright,
His naked breast glistens, now bleeds his side,
And stiff grow his arms extended wide.
Look at the nails in hands and in feet,
And the flowing streams of his blood so sweet!
Begin at the crown and search to the toe,
Nothing shall you find there but anguish and woe.

16

JESUS: (or Saint John?)	Mother and Maiden, come and see! Your son is nailed upon a tree, By hand and foot held motionless, His wounded body in distress. All over he is rent and torn; His head is wreathed about with thorn, His sides are bathed in blood, and he Is blind with blood and cannot see.
MARY:	My sweet Son, to me so dear, What have you done? Why are you here? That comely body in me at rest! That lovely mouth that I have kissed! Now on the Cross you make your nest; Dear child, for me what course is best?
JESUS:	Take this woman for my sake, John! Go, woman, with him when I am gone! I hang alone upon the cross, Without a mate, to save man loss. Play this game alone must I, For soul of man this death to die. My flesh decays, my blood-drops fall; I parch with thirst, for drink I call; They give me eisel mixed with gall: In woe for sins of man I fall. If man would love me in return, Then I could bear these pangs which burn. Father, I give you now my soul: My body dies to make Man whole. To free the sinful souls below, To dungeons down in hell I go. Soul of man, you are my mate: I will not leave you desolate While you love me, nor depart From my mother, who has my heart, For she has helped you steadfastly: And afterwards both you and she Shall come to where my Father is, And so have everlasting bliss.

17

My folk, what have I done to you,
Or in what matter injured you?
Trick me not, but answer true.
I led you out of Egypt free,
But to the Cross you now lead me:
                              My folk, etc.

Through the wilderness I led you,
Forty years in safety bred you,
With the food of angels fed you,
And at last to home I sped you:
                              My folk, etc.

What more was left for me to do?
What gift have I not given you?
                              My folk, etc.

Of food and clothes I made you free:
With eisel now you drink to me,
And with a spear you jab at me:
                              My folk, etc.

I conquered Egypt's land for you,
And killed their first-born young for you:
                              My folk, etc.

For you I cleft apart the sea,
For you, drowned Pharaoh in that sea;
And yet to princes you sell me:
                              My folk, etc.

I led you with a pillar of cloud,
But you led me to Pilate proud:
                              My folk, etc.

I fed you all with angels' food;
You strike and scourge me on the Rood:
                              My folk, etc.

Purest water I gave you all;
You drink to me with bitter gall:
                              My folk, etc.

Canaan's kings for you I beat;
You beat my head with whips of reed:
                              My folk, etc.

19

A Goodly Orison to Our Lady

Gentle mother of Jesus, holy Mary,
Light-beam of my life, beloved Lady,
I bend my knee in loyalty to you,
And all my heart-blood dedicate to you.
You are my life and hope, my spirit's light,
My sure salvation and my heart's delight.
I ought to honour you with all my might
And sing your praise in hymn by day and night.
For you have succoured me in many ways,
And taken me from hell to paradise.
My thanks to you, sweet Lady, here I give,
And ever shall so thank you while I live.
All Christian men are bound to worship you
And, much rejoicing, sing their hymns to you,
For you have loosed them from the Devil's hand,
And sent them joyful to the angels' land.
Indeed, beloved Lady, we should praise you,
Indeed abase our hearts, in love to raise you.
In bliss and brightness you surpass all womankind;
In precious life and goodness you excel mankind.
All maidens in their concourse honour you alone,
You, their flower of all, before God's holy throne.
No woman born is like you here on earth,
And heaven holds none to match you in your worth.
On high behold your throne aloft with cherubim,
With your beloved Son among the seraphim!
Before you angels blithely make their melody,
Entuned with chant and instrument alternately,
Delighting as they move and sing before you,
Unwearying as they look on and adore you.
Your bliss no mortal mind can understand,
For all God's kingdom lies within your hand.
All your company you raise to wealthy kings
With gifts of royal garments, bracelets, golden rings.[1]
Tranquillity you give them, full of sweetest bliss,
Secure from death and harm and all unhappiness.
In blossom white and red, bloom blisses there above,
And chilling snow and frost they have no knowledge of:

1. The standard tokens of nobility in the age of saga.

In that eternal summer such can never fall,
Nor do they know of weakness or any woe at all.
They honoured you on earth, their life was clean
And free from sin, and now they rest serene.
Exempt from toil and woe, carefree in heaven they dwell:
They never weep or mourn, or know the stench of hell.
With golden censers' perfume there they shall fulfil
Eternal life in harmony with angels' will.

Heart cannot feel, nor mind be well aware,
Nor mouth express, nor mortal tongue declare,
What paradisal bounties you prepare
For those who labour for you day and night.
You clothe your throng in robes of purest white,
And crown them all with crowns of golden light;
Their fair complexions show rose-red and lily-white,
And endlessly they sing in limitless delight.
Their crowns are studded all with gems as bright as fire,
And nothing being denied, they do what they desire.
With your beloved Son as king and you as Queen,
They dwell for ever free from driving wind and rain,
And ever know broad day without succeeding night,
And song without affliction, peace without a fight.
Most manifold their mirth, devoid of pain and woe.
As harping in their glee, all free delight they know!

And so, my Lady dear, we wretches long desire
That you shall fetch us forth from this creation dire.
For we can never have the utmost ecstasy
Until we join with you and honour you on high.
Gentle Mother of God, sweet Maid of choicest worth,
None like you ever was, or shall be, born on earth.
Most lofty Mother and Maiden, free from every stain,
In calm, divine repose in angels' high domain,
Where all that host of angels, every holy thing,
In speech and song acclaim you as life's fountain-spring,
They say you always give your grace and never scorn
Your worshippers, who thus are never left forlorn.
Most precious, after your beloved Son, are you;
No lie is it to say you are my soul most true.
The whole of heaven is full of your sweet bliss;
Suffused is earth with your mild-heartedness.
So mighty is your mercy and your gentleness
That those who pray for help in earnest have success.

You grant to all who plead your mercy and your grace,
Though deep their guilt and shame, and heavy their distress.
I beg you therefore, holy, heavenly Queen,
That, if it be your will, you hear my plea.

I beg you, Lady, by the greeting given
Through Gabriel to you from the King of Heaven:
I beg you also by Christ Jesu's blood,
Shed for Man's advantage on the Rood:
I beg you by the grief that filled your mind,
Standing there before him while he died,
To make me pure without and pure within,
That so I never am undone by sin:
Then loathsome Devil, devilry of every kind,
All filth abominable, I well may leave behind.
My precious life shall cleave for ever to your love,
For fortune, life itself, spring only from your love.
I labour and I murmur for your love,
And I am brought in bondage for your love,
And I have left my pleasures for your love,
And rendered you my all: beloved, think of this!
That sometimes I have crossed you, sadly I confess.
For the five wounds of Christ, show me mercy and grace,
For should you not forgive, I know that I shall be
Tormented down in hell, and burn eternally.

You watch me from above, and all from one fixed place
See where I am and what I do and give it grace.
If you had taken vengeance on my wickedness,
I know I should have lost my hope of heaven's bliss.
You have as yet condoned my sins through gentleness,
And now from every fault I hope to have release.
The pains of hell I think I never then shall have,
Once I have come to you and am your faithful slave.
Yours I am and shall be, now and evermore,
For through God's grace and yours, my life is ever sure.
My sweet beloved Lady, longing for you so,
Unless you succour me, joy shall I never know.
I pray you, be with me when I go hence,
And then especially your love dispense.
Receive my soul when from this life I onward fare,
And shield me then from death's unpitying woe and care.
Good keeping grant me if you will that I must die,

For you, and only you, my soul can prosper by,
Such wicked vices hold in slavery my soul;
And none so well as you can make these cankers whole.

Except your precious Son, I trust in you alone:
For his Name's sake, allow me life on loan!
Keep me safe from grasp of the Enemy,
Nor into hell-pain let him hurtle me!
Take hold of me yourself, for so I shall do best,
For honour falls to you if I, poor wretch, am blest.
You forsake no man for wickedness alone,
If he implores forgiveness and is prompt to atone.
It being your will, you can with ease my pain allay,
And care for me much better than I well can say.
My toil, my grief and tears, my erring sense,
All these most simply you can recompense.
In me there is no beauty to behold,
No estimable worth I dare uphold,
Yet, through your mercy spreading evermore,
Wash me clean and clothe me, I implore!
The Devil tugs me hard – no honour that to you –
And if you let him win, his joy will spring anew,
For he would never wish that you should have esteem,
Or that a man who honours you should happy seem.
You know indeed the Devil hates me through and through:
For that especially I praise and honour you.

Therefore I pray you, guide me, guard me so that he
May never torture me nor trick with phantasy.
So guide and guard me, Lady, in your gentleness,
That you may render me a share of heavenly bliss.
If much I fell from virtue, much I will amend,
Confess and to you, Lady, low in greeting bend.
Nothing shall stop me serving you if with your will
I may possess my life and my well-being still.
Before your feet I shall prostrate myself and wail;
So may my plea for quittance of my sins prevail.
My life, my love, my blood are yours, beloved Lady,
And if I dare pronounce it, you are mine, my Lady.
You have all honour in heaven and also on the earth;
To have all happiness besides well suits your worth.
And now I pray that, through Christ's charity,
Your love and blessing you may give to me.

Keep my body in all cleanliness,
That God Almighty in his gentleness
Allow me to behold you in high bliss.
And all my friends beg you in prayer today
What I have sung you in this English lay.[1]

And now I beg you by your holiness
To bring your Monk to final happiness
Who made this song on you, beloved Lady,
Gentle Mother of Jesus, holy Mary!

20

ANNUNCIATION   Holy Mary, Lady bright,
Mother of abounding might,
Heavenly Queen of feature fair!
Gabriel down from God came winging,
The Holy Spirit with him bringing
To alight within you there.
The word of God you heard and knew,
Acknowledged it with mildness due,
And calmly said, 'So let it be!'
Steadfast was your mind and true.
For the joy that then was new,
Lady, show your grace to me!

NATIVITY   Holy Mary, Mother mild,
Your Father gave you, once, a child:
Such joy again shall never be.
The savage Devil, strong and bold,
Destroyed the work of God's own mould
With an apple from the tree.
Lady, man you brought to weal,
And put the Fiend beneath your heel,
When you bore your Son to light.
For that joy's most blessed sake,
Grant me grace, that I may make
You hymns of praise with all my might.

1. To depart from the (Latin) language of prayer seems to this monk an act which must be covered by orthodox devotions!

RESURRECTION

Holy Mary, Mother of God,
Queen on earth, envoy of God,
That you should suffer with such loss!
By Judas was your offspring sold
To Jews who kept him in their hold —
They planned to kill him on the Cross.
Three days later, he arose
To life and ended all your woes:
The greatest joy you ever knew.
Lady, for that bliss begun
When you delighted in your Son,
Relieve me of my deeds untrue!

ASCENSION

Holy Mary, Maiden Mother,
Greater far than any other,
You listen to all who cry to you.
Most mighty bliss to you was given
When, there ascending into heaven,
You saw the Son who sprang from you.
On high beside our God he sits,
Ruling all, as well befits.
We may hear and we may see,
Lady, through your lofty might,
The pleasant bliss of heaven bright.
Holy Mary, plead for me!

ASSUMPTION

The fairest of the five joys given
Was when you joined your Son in heaven
Pacing toward the one you bore.
Now in heaven you are Queen
Beside your Son of lovely mien;
The Lady whom all men adore.
There in joy and lasting bliss,
Without a pause or moment's miss,
You are Queen without a doubt.
For these joys that never fail,
Lady, make my prayers prevail.
Let me never be cast out!

21

(In Latin) Here begins the song which Brother Thomas of Hales, of the order of the Minorites, composed at the instance of a young lady dedicated to God.

A maid of Christ made warm request
That I should write a lovers' lay,
That through it she might study best
Another true love to essay,
And find of men the faithfullest,
The best man known to ladies gay.
I shall not spurn the maid's behest;
But counsel her as best I may.

Maiden, here you may behold
That worldly love is spasm mad,
Beset by evils manifold,
Deceitful, weak and false and bad.
The thanes who once were fierce and bold
Have gone like wind upon the gad;
Beneath the ground they moulder cold,
Like meadow grass which withers dead.

Of human kind not one alive
Can keep on earth a constant breast,
For here abundant sorrows thrive,
Which take from man his peace and rest.
Towards his end the moments drive,
And fleeting is his earthly quest.
Then anguish and his death arrive,
Just when he hopes to prosper best.

There's none so rich and none so free
That shall not soon go hence away,
Nor is there hope in guarantee
Of gold or silver, furs of grey.
However swift, he cannot flee,
Nor win his life a single day:
Thus goes the world, as you can see,
A shadow that dissolves away.

This world is brief and all confined:
    When one man comes, another goes;
The one who led now lags behind;
    Whom loves adored, now hates oppose:
And so they wander like the blind
    Who to this world their loves dispose.
For this world's worth you see declined;
    Here virtue droops, while evil grows.

That love that cannot here abide,
    You wrongly grant it true belief,
For when its frenzied fits subside,
    You find it brittle, false, and brief,
Perverse at every time and tide.
    Yet while it lasts, there's much of grief.
But though man strive on every side,
    At last it withers like the leaf.

Man's life is short, a single throe.
    Now he loves, and now he's sad;
Now he'll come and now he'll go;
    Now he rages, now he's glad;
His love is fixed, then to and fro;
    He loves the foe he lately had.
Its truth no man can ever know;
    Whoever trusts in it is mad.

If man is rich in worldly weal,
    It makes his heart both smart and ache;
And when he fears that thieves will steal,
    His thoughts with anguish make him wake.
To keep it all he plans with zeal,
    Yet would not have his conscience quake.
What gain can come from such a deal?
    For all his profits Death will take.

Paris and Helen, where are they,
    Their loveliness and beauties bright?
Where Amadas, Edoyne, I say,
    Tristram, Iseult, all their delight?
Hector, with his strong array,
    And Caesar, rich in worldly might?
Out of the rain they've slid away,
    As sheaves glide off the sloping height.

It is as if they never were,
  Nor all the wonders of them told.
Was it not pitiful to hear
  How they were lost in griefs untold,
What miseries they suffered here?
  Now all their heat is turned to cold.
Thus friends on earth all false appear:
  To trust in them is madly bold.

If there were a noble one
  As rich as Henry, England's king,[1]
As fair to see as Absalom,
  Whose beauty there's no equalling,
Yet would his pride be quickly gone:
  It would not merit honouring.
If, maid, to lover you would come,
  Then let me tell of one true King.

Ah sweet one! If you only knew
  The beauties of this virtuous Child!
So fair he is, so bright of hue,
  So cheerful, yet of spirit mild,
Most loving and most trusty-true,
  Kind of heart, with wisdom filled;
Nor would you ever need to rue
  The time you took him for your shield.

He is the richest in the land:
  You hear it said by every mouth.
And everyone lies in his hand,
  Both east and west, and north and south.
Henry, king of all our land,
  Owes him fealty devout.
Maid, he seeks to know you and
  With such an aim he has set out.

Not land or folk does he require,
  Nor furs, nor silks, for any dower;
No need has he, nor yet desire:
  Of wealth and land he has good store.
But if you give him love entire,
  And be his lover evermore,
Then he will bring you such attire
  As king or Caesar never wore.

                1. Henry III, 1216–72.

What would you say did you behold
    A building reared by Solomon
In jasper, sapphire, finest gold,
    And many another precious stone?
Yet fairer, fairer many-fold
    Than I can tell you is the home
That shall be given you, maid, to hold,
    If you will be his plighted one.

Within true wall-moat towering free,
    Never shall it fail at all.
No miner's spade or battery
    Shall sap its base or make it fall.
There bliss and joy and song and glee
    Shall cure all woe and sweeten gall:
And, maiden, yours shall this place be,
    And every single bliss withal.

There friend from friend flees not away,
    Nor can friendship lose its right;
There hate and wrath can never stay
    In any man, nor pride, nor spite.
There all folk with the angels play,
    All joined in peace in heaven's light.
Do they not live a noble way
    Who love the Lord with all their might?

There's no man living who could see
    Our Lord in all his matchless might,
And, looking on him there, not be
    Most blissful at the noble sight.
That vision is all joy and glee,
    An endless day without a night.
Would it not, maid, be ecstasy
    To dwell with such a worthy knight?

More rich than gold or furs in dower
    One treasure is, his sayings tell.
He bids you love and keep your bower,
    Desires you guard your virtue well
From robbers', thieves', and lechers' power.
    In vigilance and care excel,
For you are sweeter than a flower
    While you keep your citadel.

From distant place this gem is borne;
    No better is in heaven's domain.
Before all virtues it is worn,
    And it can heal all lovers' pain.
Ah! Fortunate the maidens born
    Who can this holy state maintain!
But once you lose it, then forlorn,
    You never win it back again.

This gem-stone now to you I name:
    'Maidenhood' its title is.
It is a single precious gem,
    Which, best of all, bears off the prize,
And takes you clean and pure of fame
    Into the bliss of paradise.
Guard it beneath your underhem,
    And stay more sweet than any spice.

What say you of the jewels you see
    Which tend to virtue or to grace?
When amethyst, chalcedony,
    Amber, topaz, sapphire's blaze,
Jasper, sardonyx you see,
    Beryl, emerald, chrysoprase?
Among all precious jewellery,
    Maidenhood has highest place.

Maiden, as I said, I hold
    The gem of all your bower, your jewel,
More pure of hue a hundredfold
    Than all I named, more beautiful.
For it is worked in heavenly gold,
    And of the finest love is full.
Let all preserve its sheen untold,
    In heaven's bower most wonderful.

Since you ask that I advise
    And choose a loving mate for you,
I'll speak as best I can devise,
    And pick the finest that I know.
So were it not a wicked vice,
    When free to choose one man from two,
Needlessly to be unwise,
    And take the worse, the good let go?

Maiden, this rhyme to you I send
   Without a seal on any part:[1]
Unroll it, as I recommend,
   And learn the verses well by heart,
And by its means your grace extend;
   And teach to other maids its art.
Whoever knows it to the end,
   Much good to her it will impart.

When longing comes to where you lie,
   Draw out the scroll of this my writ,
And sweetly sing melodiously,
   And do as you are bid by it.
God sends you greeting: so may he
   Be gracious to you every whit,
And grant you at his bridal be,[2]
   On high in heaven where he sits.

And may he have fair destiny
   Who wrote this work, made song of it!

22

Adam lay in bondage,
Bound in fetters strong;
Four thousand winters
Thought he not too long:
And all was for an apple,
An apple that he took,
As holy men find written
In their holy book.

Had the apple not been taken,
The apple taken been,
Never would Our Lady
Have been Heaven's Queen.
Blessed be the time
That apple taken was!
Therefore we must sing,
'Deo gracias!'

1. i.e. it is not a poem secretly addressed to one loved with earthly passion.
2. See 'Pearl', stanza 66, page 163.

23[1]

Love made firm in Christ shall live for ever;
And truly, weal or woe shall shake it never;
Night moves to day, and travel ends in rest;
Love as I say, and company the blest.

Love yearns for the beloved with pure desire;
Love is like imperishable fire.
Love purges sin; love brings us home to bliss;
Love sings of joy; love wins the kingly kiss.

On earth men blench and sicken at love's sway,
But love is throned in heaven: though hard the way,
Love brings us near that bed of rare delight
Where Christ and soul of man at last unite.

Love hotter than burning coals, love ever the same,
Love undeceivable, who can resist its flame?
Love lifts us heavenward, comforted and whole;
Incomparable, bears Christ into the soul.

Study this love to win immortal life;
Give all your thought to him who ends your strife;
Cleave to his heart in time of threatening woe;
Win and possess him, ever love him so.

Your love, my life-redeemer, Jesu, lend me;
Be my sole aim, to your high passion bend me.
Could my soul hear and catch your anthem-song,
Cares go, and welcome, love for which I long!

Your love is endless; burn my soul in it,
Till nothing can allay its living heat;
So mould my mind and set it with your hand,
That love of worldly joys I may withstand.

If earthly thing my love and will admit,
And I account it joy, possessing it,
Such loss of love, such torment, I must dread,
For sorrow is my lot when soul is dead.

Like mowing grass, that now is fair and green,
Now fades, is all the joy that men have seen.
Such is this world until the ending day;
Escape its toils and troubles, no man may.

1. The original is in mono-rhyming quatrains, with internal rhyming.

Love only love, and hate the filth of sin;
Give Christ your soul, that we may dwell within;
For as he bought it, sought it, seeks it, so
Shall you have bliss, and heaven in you grow.

The nature of love is this: where it is true,
It stays for ever and will not change for new.
Who holds, or once possessed, love in his mind,
Is saved from care, and heart's delight shall find.

Stand with the angels; give the Lord your love,
And do not barter here your joys above;
The powers that menace love, abhor them well;
Yet love is strong as death and firm as hell.

Love is no burden; cheers both age and youth;
Is free of anguish, lovers say in truth.
Wine to the soul, love strength and valour imparts;
All's profit to those who hold it in their hearts.

Love is God's darling; binds both blood and bone;
And is man's sweetest gain. If love alone
Be our delight, I know no better aim;
My loved one and myself become the same.

But fleshly love is like a flower in May,
And scarcely lasts an hour in the day:
And then desire and joy and pride lament
In lasting woe their sad predicament.

Body to body in sin, their souls in fear,
Mankind shall judge them; if they then appear
As sinful, by their mode of life abhorred,
Hell shall receive them, dark be their reward.

The great and rich shall grieve when hellish flames
Redeem in fire their wicked deeds and shames.
But if you long for love, in measure sing
To Christ, whose love prevails in everything.

I seek that face of beauty past belief;
Only immortal love can ease my grief;
To see him, or to know him, ends all pain,
Turns mourning song to brightest glad refrain.

They live in joy who love that sweetest Child:
Jesu it is, of all most meek and mild.
Though sinful, one who loves him shall not fear;
Evil and wrath of God shall not come near.

I love to speak of him whose sweetness charms
My heart till it must burst, and cures all harms;
Whose unforgettable love snares all my thought,
Whose bleeding hands and feet my soul have bought.

My heart, beholding him, breaks with desire.
Fair is the love that keeps its sacred fire,
That strengthens grace though robbing us of rest:
Of all things on the earth this love is best.

No wonder I lament the gallows-tree,
Where Christ was nailed and beaten wickedly.
Heart aches to ponder on his tender cries:
Leave sin, O Man, who prompts such sacrifice.

Love's sweetness is beyond man's power to tell;
Who loves with longing, God protects from hell.
O endless joy, that those who dwell in love
Shall from their foes be saved by God above!

Jesu, who makes the day from darkness spring,
Guard us, for we acknowledge you as King.
O everlasting love whom we adore,
Give us grace to love you evermore!

Poems of Sin and Death

Spring redeems: winter punishes. As the fixed medieval world was warmed by the returning sun in spring, nature was renewed in the all-but-universal redemption. In this manifestation of God man's soul could share, but not his flesh, once winter had settled in it. For as, in nature's winter, God seemed to have withdrawn from an unaccommodated world, so, in the late life of man, God's functions in the failing body seemed attenuated. Man gravely feared this threatened desertion. His erring soul, watching in horror the decay of its fleshly home, was haunted by memories of sinful joy in its pride of life, taunted by only too poignant visions of never-to-be-had heavenly blisses. In the sick man's delirium, demons licensed to be hungry for sinners panted and writhed just below the crust of earth. 'The true fiend governs in the name of God' (Robert Graves).

To be fair to the spirit of the Middle Ages, it must be said that its sermons and poems usually celebrate bodily decay as the black reverse to the white ideal of spiritual immortality. But bodily decay and the earthly sin associated with it could be experienced or witnessed by both laity and clergy; while immortality was an intangible object of yearning to the laity, and to the clergy, besides this, an abstract subject of theological speculation. Moreover, the portrayal of vice provides material for a wider range of moral tales than the portrayal of virtue: reforming zeal habitually concerns itself with the dark side of life. Hence the great theocratic age of England sends down the centuries an image of a society dominated by Death the Skeleton. In cathedral sculpture and painting, in play, poem, and sermon, he is there to affront the will-to-life of the natural man. He is God's agent in the divine scheme. He warns man and conducts him to the grave: he is the leveller, reducing to non-effect princes in their pomp and power, warriors in their strength and courage, women in their pride and beauty. And round these three main representatives of humanity in bondage to death, the mendicant preachers in particular painted in sinners of every kind from all walks of life.

The gentle, sunny extroversion of Chaucer, and the undue emphasis laid on the few surviving love-poems of the Middle Ages, have perhaps tended to leave in the public mind too rosy a picture of the time. The conditions in which most of the people lived, and the actual experience of calamities like the Black Death, which killed one-third of the population, are two of many matters which, when weighed against modern problems such as how to make use of leisure or prevent use of the hydrogen bomb, seem to justify the medieval preoccupation with doom. After all, doom in its most concrete form, death, was everywhere. Its ubiquitousness induced in the priestly writers, as it did in later poets, like Villon, or those of the First World War, a certain familiarity with, not to say callousness in contemplation of, the physical show of death's mystery.

So it is that this section contains only a few of the very many poems concerned with the four last things (Death, Judgement, Hell, and Heaven): penitence, when it comes, has a panic-stricken, eleventh-hour urgency. These poems are each a part of the monody of their age, in which the sputtering flesh oozes off the bone, and, before the first clods thud on the coffin lid, the soul is hurried howling into hell.

The first poem is a song, the music for which is printed in *Early Bodleian Music*. It is one of the oldest songs in English, and may well be older than 'Sumer is i-cumen in'. The two short pieces so full of dread, which follow, are also early ones, probably from the beginning of the thirteenth century, although one is on a manuscript of later date. 'The Life of this World' conveys a pagan terror of existence and death, of a kind with which readers of Old English will be familiar. This horror of a reasonless scheme dominated by black night and dark wind found, with the arrival of Christianity, a decorous modulation into a scarcely less terrified contemplation of the fate of the body under the new dispensation, and it is often only as an afterthought that it is admitted that the soul may be excused the body's destiny. In poem no. 27, self-righteousness joins with that terror to produce a kind of morbid glorying in death, which the marked rhythm exalts to a spell. The Address of the Soul to the Body is a common theme.

The 'Signs of Death', poem no. 28, represents a popular thirteenth-century genre, the original of which, in Latin, was thought to have been the work of Saint Jerome. But experience of death, which was common, would lead to the signs of it being catalogued in popular lore. The Hostess knew how to tell that Falstaff was dying – 'His nose was as sharp as a pen' (cited by Carleton Brown).

No. 29 is the earliest surviving poem written in a ten-line stanza with only two rhymes (as in the last three stanzas of the present translation). The number of manuscripts on which it exists, or is quoted, proves its popularity. With this poem is ushered in the note of social criticism: poets like its writer, and preachers like John Bromyard, the great Dominican whose *Summa Predicantia*, G. R. Owst suggests, 'presents us with the gathered fruit of Mendicant preaching', were bound to communicate the subversive message inherent in Christianity, and knew that they could rely on God to act upon it in the next world. No wonder that works which reminded the great of their servitude to death, and by inference told the poor that their suffering would be recompensed hereafter, were popular. Poem no. 32, on the well-known 'Ubi Sunt' motif, underlines the social message, too, but balances the vision of judgement on the high and mighty with a pleasant picture of the Christian knight battling his way to heaven. The poet is human enough to describe fairly the ceremonial round of castle pleasure, but holds his sympathy sufficiently in check to single out its un-Christian qualities.

No. 33, another early-thirteenth-century poem, is a formal confession addressed to the Virgin Mary as intercessor. It is typical of one aspect of religious teaching that the penitent of the poem, whose fear is so forcibly and even comically described in the fourth stanza, should have committed only the warm sins of the gay life. Poem no. 30 illustrates the moralist's desire to see the life of man in terms of a set progress, each step in which is harmonized to the world-weary sense of futility found in Ecclesiastes. In the original, the sixth stage switches inexplicably into the first person.

24

Merry it is while summer lasts,
    With birds in song;
But now there threaten windy blasts
    And tempests strong.
Ah! but the night is long,
    And I, being done such wrong,
Sorrow and mourn and fast.

25

The life of this world
Is governed by wind,
Weeping, darkness
    And pangs.
Wind-blown we bloom,
Wind-blown decay;
With weeping we come
And so pass away.
    In pangs we start,
    In pangs we end;
    In dread we stay
    And in dread depart.

26

When the turf is your tower
And the pit is your bower,
The worms shall note
Your skin and white throat.
What help to you then
That the world is won?

27

Now that man is hale and whole,
Evil comes and twists his soul;
Then a call goes out for priest,
Who urges him to turn to Christ.
When the priest has spent his breath,
Man is seized by dreadful death.
They wrap him in a filthy clout,
And in a vault they lay him out.
In the morning, south and north,
They take the rotting body forth,
Dig in pit or under stone,
And bury deep that giddy bone.

Says soul to corpse, 'Alas the day
I lodged in you for earthly stay!
No Friday fasting till midday,
No giving alms on Saturday,
No going to church on sabbath day,

No Christian deeds on any day!
Though proud as proud you here became,
Being fair of face and high in fame,
You'll house in earth, by worms be gnawed,
By lovers of the good abhorred.'

28

When my eyes are fogged
And my ears are clogged
And my nose turns cold
And my tongue's back rolled
And my cheeks slacken
And my lips blacken
And my mouth blubbers
And my spittle slobbers
And my hair stands up
And my heart-beats droop
And my hands quiver
And my feet stiffen, –
All too late, all too late,
When the bier is at the gate!

Then I shall go
From bed to floor,
From floor to shroud,
From shroud to bier,
From bier to pit
And be shut in it.

Then lies my house upon my nose,
And all my care for this world goes.

29

Long life, O Man, you hope to gain,
Till flattened by a cunning wrench.
Your temperate weather turns to rain,
Your sun is strangely made to blench;
So here's a thought your teeth should clench:
'All greenness comes to withering.'
Alas! There is no queen or king
Whom draught of Death shall fail to drench:
Before you tumble off your bench,
    All sinning quench!

There's none so strong, or tough, or keen
That he can dodge Death's wither-clench:
Young and old and bright of sheen,
All, all he shatters with his strength.
Swift and fearful is his wrench:
Before it every man must quail.
Alas! No tears or prayers prevail,
No bribes, or guile, or doctor's drink;
So, Man, let sin and pleasure stink!
      Do well, so think!

Go by Solomon the Wise,
O Man, and prosperously do;
Follow his teaching and advice,
Then you never shall misdo,
Whatever ending comes to you.
Dreading much to pay the price,
Alas! You think good deeds suffice
To bring long life and bliss to you –
But Death is lurking by your shoe
      To run you through!

Consider, Man, how you should go,
And study in what plight you're thrown:
In filth you're sown, in filth you grow,
And worms shall eat you for their own.
Three days of bliss you've hardly known
On earth, and all your life is woe.
Alas! By Death you're dragged below,
Just when you thought to stay on throne!
You'll find your luck to misery grown,
      Your joy to moan.

By world and wealth you're led astray;
They are your enemies, I know.
They sleek you with their gaudies gay,
To get you gripped in deathly throe.
Therefore, Man, let pleasure go,
And earn your bliss another day.
Alas! You yield in shameful way
Just once or twice, to pleasures low,
And earn your everlasting woe.
      Man, do not so!

30

The Ten Ages of Man

10 Times of the Day
The Life of Man Runs Out in 10 Stops on Our Way
10 Spokes that Turn Ay

1 Woeful wretch you are to the sight,
Of all the creatures least in might.

2 All this world you turn to play:
The more you play, the more you may.

3 Wealth makes man at others gape,
For to the rich, men bow and scrape.

4 Now you have found the thing you sought:
Beware, for it continues not.

5 Strong you were, now fails your might:
You're heavy now, who once were light.

6 All your life you sorrowed and cared,
For soon comes Death, and none is spared.

7 Wisdom you have in tongue and mind:
How you have lived, you soon shall find.

8 This world's goods shall now forsake you,
For Death has come, and he will take you.

9 Men and women all end so:
Easy they come, and easy go.

10 For life you have no need to care
When worms have got you for their fare.

31

Hard it is to flit
From earthly joy to pit;
Harder still to miss
Heavenly kingdom's bliss;
Hardest of all to go
To everlasting woe.
Our heart's delight gone, all,
And all our gladness turned to gall.
The crown of our head is fallen away:
That ever we sinned, alas the day!

32

'Ubi Sunt qui ante Nos Fuerunt?'

Where are those who lived before?
Who chased with hawk and hound of yore,
   Possessing fields and woods?
The noble ladies in their bowers,
Complexions bright, and sweet as flowers,
   And gold-embroidered snoods?

They ate and drank with mirth and song,
And revels lit their lives along;
   And men came kneeling low.
They bore themselves too proudly high,
And in the twinkling of an eye
   Their souls were lost in woe.

Where is the laughter and the song
Of all the proud, skirt-trailing young?
   And where the hawk and hound?
Gone is all their happiness;
Their joy has turned to wretchedness
   And agonies profound.

On earth they had all heaven's desire,
But now they lie in hellish fire,
   The fire that burns for ever.
Long that 'ever' for men to bear,
And long their bondage to despair;
   And they escape it never.

Be wise, O Man, and gladly know
A little torment here below;
   Shrink from your pleasures often.
And when you suffer bitter pain,
Consider well your heavenly gain,
   And earthly pangs shall soften.

If the Devil, loathsome hound,
Has not hurled you to the ground
   With wicked words or charms,
Stand firm, and never fall again
Before a little blast of bane;
   And be God's knight-at-arms.

Uplift the cross upon your stave,
And think of him who gladly gave
  A life most precious held.
Return the gift he made to you,
And with avenging rod pursue
  Until that foe is quelled.

Let right believing be your shield
While you battle on that field,
  To strengthen heart and hand.
Ward off your foe with point of staff,
And conquer him on God's behalf;
  So win the happy land.

For there the daytime knows no night,
And endlessly God's strength and might
  Deal death to every foe.
And God himself gives every life
Peace and rest devoid of strife,
  And solace free from woe.

Maiden Mother, Heavenly Queen,
Shield us from the Devil's spleen!
  For so you can and should.
Give us strength all sin to shun,
That we may ever behold your Son
  In high beatitude!

33

Holy Lady Mary, Mother, Maid,
Guide me, for I lack your prudent aid!
Too long a wretched, useless life I led,
And when I think of it, I shake with dread.

A host of evils holds me hard confined,
Sins small, sins great, and sins of every kind.
By day and night I yearn and strive to amend:
Some grace to me may God in heaven send!

Sleep steals my life, a half of it or more.
Away! Too late this sleeping I abhor,
Though when I die, I sleep for evermore.
O warier man than I, hear this my lore!

Too long he sleeps who never will awake!
Aware of Judgement Day, a man should shake
His evils off, and give for goodness' sake;
Or when he dies, his breeches-belt will quake.

Sleep stole away my life before I knew;
And now too well my eye can see it true.
My hair, once brown, is white – some dyeing brew: –
My sanguine face has taken another hue.

Of old I sinned, and sinned in deed and word,
Sometimes in bed and sometimes at the board;
Drank wine in plenty, seldom from the ford;
And spent too much, too little kept in hoard.

The hoard I reckon good is virtuous deed:
The naked, clothe them, and the hungry, feed;
The witless, teach them wise men's words to heed;
And love and dread almighty God indeed.

Since first I could do harm, I sinned my fill;
In deed, with mouth, with all my limbs, did ill.
My grief for many sins, which now I spill,
Should earlier have flowed, with Christ's good will.

Merciful Mother, my temper so dispose
That love for God and man my spirit knows;
That I may curb my flesh and shame my foes,
And feed on meekness till my life shall close.

Holy Mary, hear these sins of mine
And bear my message to your Son divine,
Whose flesh and blood, through water, bread, and wine.
To shield us from hell's agonies combine.

Yes, I have overdrunk and overfed,
Been too well shod and in proud clothes have spread.
I heard God's voice, but cared not what I said:
I think of all these things and shake with dread.[1]

---

1. It was hard to resist making this stanza the ninth, and so improving the order of the poem.

Miscellaneous Religious Poems

The medieval preacher's habit of occasionally versifying what he wished to teach is further exemplified by the poems in this section. Of many metrical versions of the Ten Commandments, the one included, no. 34, is perhaps the earliest surviving poem. As one would expect, the writer does not wish to remind his flock that the law of God as delivered by Moses forbade the making of images, but the omission of the injunction against stealing is more curious, and is not repeated in other and later versions. The author conforms to medieval custom in accompanying the giving of the law with precise description of the fate of those who ignore it, and of those who follow it. The interesting little poem of moral character, 'The Covetous Man', nicely signalizes the True Church's contempt of earthly riches, and would appear to be appropriate in a mendicant preacher's repertoire.

The two short poems, nos. 36 and 37, have a strong personal atmosphere, but in fact the second is a direct translation from the *Confessions* of Saint Augustine; its relevance to the problem of faith, and simple, vivid dramatization of that problem, much commend it: the translator's little poem seems even more memorable than the prose of the original. Poem no. 36, as one would expect from its praise of the Minorites, is from a manuscript to which Carleton Brown assigns a Franciscan origin. That indicates that the poem constitutes a poetic advertisement of the Order, written by one within the fold, rather than the personal yearning of a potential convert.

'The Thrush and the Nightingale' survives on a Digby manuscript which is second only to MS. Harley 2253 for the value of what it has preserved of thirteenth-century poetry (see poems nos. 32, 54, 95, 96). The importance of the theme of Woman makes it an essential choice for this collection, although it is no more than a versified debate. The logic of the Nightingale's winning case will not bear examination; but the scales are weighted in favour of the love-bird from the start, because every educated listener would know that the Thrush was the paradigm of Contention.

The remaining poems in the section are from the famous early fifteenth-century manuscript, Sloane 2593. They are all carols, and combine a fine moral and religious sense with splendid musical *élan*. In the original, the last line of each stanza rhymes with both lines of the couplet refrain, as in the translation of nos. 41 and 42. It thus provides a leading sound as well as a leading note for the refrain to begin.

34

The Ten Commandments

One God in worship entertain;
Never take his name in vain;
Keep and guard your holy day;
To father and mother, honour pay;
Murder of men, put out of mind;
Never sin with womankind;
False oath, swear not;
False witness, bear not;
For wife of neighbour, see you never lust;
For goods of neighbour, have no greed unjust.

Good are these commandments ten:
Keep them strictly, all you men!
He who will not keep them well
Shall go down to deepest hell.
He who keeps them right
Shall go to heaven bright.

35

The Covetous Man

He's all alone and has no other;
No son, no sister and no brother.
He's no child of good upbringing;
To his work he's always clinging.
He only thinks about himself,
And sweats and toils for private pelf.
Day and night awake at tilth.
He lets his soul be clad in filth.

36

No longer will I wicked be!
All worldly wealth shall go from me,
Fantastic clothes and frantic glee.
    Meek be my attire;
Knotted shall my girdle be:
    I will become a friar.

A Minorite I will become;
All lechery I then will shun.
To Jesus Christ I mean to come,
    And serve in holy kirk,
And watch when offices are sung,
    And carry out God's work.

This shall I do, and all things good,
For him who bought us on the Rood.
From his side ran down the blood –
    He bought us grievously.
I count him more than mad who would
    Persist in lechery.

37

Lord, you called to me,
And I gave no reply
But slowly, sleepily:
'Wait a while yet! Wait a little!'
But 'yet' and 'yet' goes on and on,
And 'wait a little' grows too long.

38

The Thrush and the Nightingale

Summer's here with love again,[1]
With blossom and with birds' refrain
    From hazel bushes springing.
Dew is dropping in the dale
And, longing like the nightingale,
    The birds are gladly singing.

1. A conventional opening: see no. 84.

I heard a wordy battle flow –
On one side joy, the other woe –
   Between two birds I knew.
One praised women for their good.
But shame the sex the other would:
   Their strife I tell to you.

The one was Nightingale by name,
And he would shield them all from shame
   And safe from injury.
The thrush declared that night and day
Women go the Devil's way
   And keep him company;

For every man who would believe
And trust in women, they deceive,
   Though fair and mild of mien;
False and fickle, everywhere
They bring distress, and better it were
   If they had never been.

NIGHTINGALE: 'To censure ladies is a shame,
For they are kind and fair of fame:
   Desist, I beg of you.
For there was never breach so strong
That man pursuing right or wrong
   Could not at last break through.

'They cheer the angry, noble or base,
With pleasing pastime and with grace.
   Woman was once created
As man's companion: how could earth
Be anything without her birth,
   Or man so sweetly mated?'

THRUSH: 'No praise of women I report,
For I affirm them false in thought
   And know that they will cheat;
For though they're beautiful, their mind
Is false and faithless, and I find
   Them prone to act deceit.

'King Alexander censured them –
He the prince of stratagem
   And first in wealth and fame;
And I could tell a hundredfold

Of rich and powerful men of old
   Whom women brought to shame.'

This speech enraged the Nightingale.

NIGHTINGALE: 'You seem most loath to tell the tale
   Of all those heroes' shame!
A thousand ladies I could show
And none there sitting in a row
   Would be of evil fame.

'Modest and mild of heart are all;
And shielded by their bower wall,
   They're safe from shame and snare;
The sweetest things to fold in arms
For men delighting in their charms! –
   Bird, are you not aware?'

THRUSH: 'What! Me aware, my gentle bird?
I've been in bower and often stirred
   Those ladies to my will.
They'll do a sinful secret deed
For slight reward, and so with speed
   Their souls they help to kill.

'I think you're lying now, my bird,
For though you're meek and mild of word,
   Your wilful utterance palls.
I name to you the primal man,
Adam, who our race began:
   He found women false.'

NIGHTINGALE: 'Thrush, it seems you're either mad
Or know of nothing else but bad
   To slander women so!
They have true courtliness at heart,
And sweetly use love's secret art,
   Most wonderful to know.

'Man's highest bliss in earthly state
Is when a woman takes her mate
   And twines him in her arms.
To slander ladies is a shame!
I'll banish you for laying blame
   On those who have such charms.'

To you I gave the heavenly crown,
But you give me a thorny crown.

                    My folk, etc.

I honoured you most worthily,
But on the Cross you now hang me:
    My folk, what have I done to you,
    Or in what matter injured you?
    Trick me not, but answer true!

Poems of Adoration

In the Middle Ages, the spiritual exercises of contemplation and self-surrender to deity produced a special manifestation. And although this may not be the place to question why the adoration of the Virgin became a particularly exalted activity, it may well be useful to emphasize some interesting juxtapositions. The remnants of hard-dying paganism and esoteric heresies like Catharism, the one supported by a rich folk-lore and the other by oriental mystical practices, existed side by side with a Church whose doctrines tended to become narrower and more rigid as the period developed towards the Renaissance. The Green Man and the Queen of Heaven jostled in the approach to paradise; something of his passion rubbed off on her, something of her purity on him. In poems of courtly love, celebration of the beloved often dallies with the prolonged frustration of desire, while in poems of mystical adoration, the fecundity of the Virgin is celebrated in terms as burning as those which extol her maidenhood. But in a society in which perhaps most lived in a state of serfdom, while another numerous group aspired to live in continent retreat, it was the Queen of Heaven, her claims supported by authority, who left the bigger legacy to posterity, in spite of the dualism of human nature.

The signs of the Virgin's triumph are to be found almost wherever medieval art crystallized idea or emotion. In the poems of adoration addressed to her, critics have detected a quality which, for want of a subtler word, has been called 'erotic'. But even when 'mysticism' is added to 'erotic', the expression of the delicate fusion of the female principle with tender holiness, by which those poems subsist, seems to be inadequately described. Perhaps, in a deep and simple sense, the world of passion is indivisible; so it follows that the language of passion is a unified one, too. At any rate, the sacred love-passion directed to the Virgin, or to her Son, yearning in terms of ecstasy for mystic union, was tongued with the same poetic equipment as that by means of which minstrels familiarized listeners with the longing of Sir Lancelot for Guinevere.

Adoration is common to all times, but the kind of mystical adoration which is associated with medieval expression emerges only in the fourteenth century. The lyric sweetness, repetitiousness, and poor versifying of no. 19 are typical of early thirteenth-century writing: urgency of plea and panegyric modify any conception of form which the priestly poet may have had. But no. 23, in which a burning love of man for Christ makes doctrinal points and worldly impulses alike irrelevant, reveals the true mystical passion. This poem has been attributed to Richard Rolle of Hampole, who died in 1349; lines 1–60 are a direct translation of his 'Incendium Amoris'. Although Rolle had been prepared for the priesthood, he never took orders, but set up as a recluse in Yorkshire. His passionate rather than intellectual or practical impulse seems to have appealed especially to women, who formed the main body of his patrons and admirers – yet another instance of the penchant of cultured ladies for embracing heterodoxy in the Middle Ages. By some, Rolle was regarded as a saint, and marvellous tales about him circulated in his lifetime. He could apparently discourse with his followers whilst writing of other matters, and such was his power of concentration that friends could take off, mend, and replace his clothes without his noticing. A comparison of this poem with the secular love-poem no. 54 reinforces the point made in the previous paragraph.

Although they are not in this section, poems nos. 78 and 82, from the Harley Lyrics, form a useful contrast to the three just mentioned, because they are concerned with adoration in a way that admits doctrine and supplication as well as passion. More shapely than poems of the early thirteenth century, and more balanced than those of the fourteenth, they show religious poetry in the courtly mode at its best.

Poem no. 20, from the early thirteenth century, shows how the dependence of a sacred poem on a fixed doctrinal progression can give it lyric form. The poet's scheme of allotting one complex stanza to each of the Five Joys of the Virgin gives him both movement and climax, which no. 19 lacks. The fame of the short song in praise of the Virgin, no. 22, which dates from the early fifteenth century, gives the excuse for presenting it here in barely 'translated' form.

The fourteenth-century poet of no. 18 nicely points the interdependence of sacred and secular lyric by pleading to be given God's help with a phrase which he overtly borrows from the language of courtly love. The reneguing and reaffirmation of faith in the last stanza but one give the poem a strong personal touch: this makes a welcome contrast to the naïve orthodoxy which tends to dominate medieval poetry. The poem survives most tenuously, having been written, states Carleton Brown, 'in pencil on a page left blank at the end of the text of Vegetius, *De Re Militari*'.

Poem no. 21 has already been discussed on page 15.

18

All other love is like the moon,
Which grows and shrinks like flower on plain;
Like bud that blooms and withers soon;
Like passing day that ends in rain.

All other love begins in bliss
And ends in tears and suffering:
No love can salve us all but this,
The love that rests in heaven's King.

For ever green, renewed again,
For ever full, it never pales.
It ever sweetens, free from pain,
Continues always, never fails.

All other love I fled for this:
Tell me, tell me, where you lie!
'In Mary, tender, full of bliss,
And yet still more in Christ, live I.'

I found not you, but Christ found me:
Hold me to you with might and main!
And grant that my love steadfast be,
For fear it quickly change again.

And yet – and yet – my heart is sore;
I feel it gushing out my blood.
God leave my side? I care no more –
Still, his will to me be good!

Alas! What should I do in Rome?
I say in words of courtly love:
'Man's word undoes me with its doom,
Unless he help who sits above.'

THRUSH: 'Nightingale, you do me wrong
To banish me when all my song
    Was urging of the right.
I testify to Sir Gawain,
Whom Jesus Christ gave might and main
    And valour for the fight.

'However far and wide he went,
He never failed in true intent
    By day or yet by night.'

NIGHTINGALE: 'Bird, for that untruthful word,
Your utterance shall be widely heard,
    So off with you! Take flight!

'I sojourn here by lawful right,
In orchard and in garden bright,
    And here my songs I sing.
Of women I've known but kindly word
Of grace and courtesy, and heard
    Of blisses that they bring.

'Delight is theirs without an end,
They tell me: I tell you, my friend,
    They live in sweet desire.
Bird, you sit on hazel bough:
You slandered them, you'll suffer now!
    I'll spread your tales, you liar!'

THRUSH: 'They're spread abroad, I know it well;
Who doesn't know them, go and tell:
    My tales are hardly new.
Listen, bird, to my advice:
You haven't noticed half their vice;
    I'll tell you what they do.

'Think how the queen of Constantine
Found something filthy fair and fine:
    (Regret she later knew!)
She loved a cripple whom she fed[1]

---

1. A number of old oriental tales tell of unfaithful queens whose lovers were deformed. The explanation is either Platonic (ugliness = vice), or that monsters were believed to have prodigious sexual power. Or scholiasts might interpret this tale as an *exemplum*, warning of the danger of Christian charity (in feeding and housing the cripple) being perverted to lust.

And hid within her royal bed.
Just see if women are true!'

NIGHTINGALE: 'Thrush, your tale is wholly wrong,
For as I always say in song,
  And men know far and wide,
When women to shady woods are drawn,
They're brighter than the brilliant dawn
  At height of summer-tide.

'If you come here to hostile ground
They'll shut you up, in prison bound,
  And there you shall remain.
The lying tales your lips let fall,
There you shall unsay them all,
  And live in utter shame.'

THRUSH: 'Nightingale, your speech is free:
You say that women'll ruin me –
  Curse them, young and old!
The holy book is swift to show
How women brought so many low
  Who once were proud and bold.

'Think of Samson, brave and strong,
To whom his wife did such a wrong;
  For him she took a price.
Jesus said ill-gotten gain
Was worst for one who would attain
  To bliss of paradise.'

Then said to him the Nightingale,

NIGHTINGALE: 'Well, bird, that sounds a likely tale!
  Attend to what I say.
Woman's a flower of lasting grace,
And highest praised in every place,
  And lovely her array.

'There's not on earth a better leech,
So mild of thought and fair of speech,
  To heal man's aching sore.
Bird, you pull apart my thought,
But shall not win with your retort.
  Such evil, do no more!'

THRUSH: 'Nightingale, you are unwise
To put on women such a price;
    Your profit will be lean;
For in a hundred, hardly five
Of all the wives and maids alive
    Continue pure and clean,

'And do no harm in any place,
And bring no men to vile disgrace,
    We know with certainty.
But though we sit in wordy strife
About the fame of maid and wife,
    The truth you'll never see.'

NIGHTINGALE: 'Your words have now confounded you!
Through whom was all this world made new? –
    A Maiden meek and mild,
Who bore in Bethlehem a Son.
He sprang from her a holy one
    Who tames all beings wild.

'She knew of neither sin nor shame,
And truly, Mary was her name:
    May Christ be all her shield!
Bird, for slanders that you wove,
I ban you from this wooded grove,
    So go into the field!'

THRUSH: 'Nightingale, my mind was mad,
Or else I thought of only bad
    In this our wordy war.
I see that I am overcome
Through her who bore that holy Son;
    Five wounds he suffered sore.

'I promise by his holy name
That of a wife's or maiden's fame
    No harm I'll ever say.
I'll leave your land at once, I swear,
And where I go, I do not care:
    I'll simply fly away.'

39

The man who would the truth tell,
With mighty lords he may not dwell.
In histories which wise men tell,
   Truth is given a pauper's state.

   God be with truth, wherever he be!
   I wish he were in this country.

In ladies' bowers he enters not;
In those truth dare not set a foot.
And though he would, he dare not put
   His head among the high and great.

   God be with truth, etc.

The lawyers will not give him space,
For truth they loathe in any place:
It seems to me they lack all grace
   In valuing truth at such a rate.

   God be with truth, etc.

In holy church he has no pew;
There each in turn bids him adieu;
For truth my heart is filled with rue
   That he should be so desolate.

   God be with truth, etc.

As for divines, who should be good,
I'd think truth mad to join that brood,
Because they'd tear his coat and hood,
   And chase him naked from their gate.

   God be with truth, etc.

The man who would this truth find
Should seek the bosom of Mary kind,
For there indeed he is enshrined
   And evermore inviolate.

   God be with truth, wherever he be!
   I wish he were in this country.

40

Though you be king of tower and town,
Though you be king and wear the crown,
I count for nothing your renown,
    Unless you mend your sinful ways.

    Sinful man, I say, awake!
    Amend your ways, for God's own sake.

What you have here is other men's;
So shall it be when you go hence:
Your soul shall pay for all your sins,
    Unless you mend your sinful ways.

    Sinful man, etc.

Although you be both stout and strong,
And have done many people wrong,
'Alas, Alas!' shall be your song,
    Unless you mend your sinful ways.

    Sinful man, etc.

Beware lest on the way you slither,
For you shall slide you know not whither;
Body and soul shall go together
    Unless you mend your sinful ways.

    Sinful man, etc.

Carry not your head too high
In pomp and pride and villainy!
In hell you shall be hanged on high,
    Unless you mend your sinful ways.

    Sinful man, I say, awake!
    Amend your ways, for God's own sake.

41

Pride is out and pride is in,
And pride is root of every sin,
And pride will always fight to win,
    Till he has brought a man to woe.

    Man, beware, or fall in woe:
    Consider pride, and let it go.

Lucifer was angel-bright,
A conqueror of power and might;
But through his pride he lost his light,
    And fell to everlasting woe.

    Man, beware, etc.

If you think that swear-words roared
Or fashionable clothes afford
You rights to be a king or lord,
    Little it shall avail you so.

    Man, beware, etc.

When to church at last you glide,
Worms shall burrow through your side,
And little shall avail your pride
    Or any other vice you show.

    Man, beware, etc.

Pray to Christ with bloody side
And other gashes cruel and wide,
That so he may forgive your pride
    And all your sinning here below.

    Man, beware, or fall in woe:
    Consider pride, and let it go.

42

Blowing was made for sport and game;
Blowing engenders evil fame;
And so I do not count it shame
    To bear a horn and blow it not.

    I hold him sound and wisely taught
    Who bears his horn but blows it not.

Horns are made both loud and shrill:
At the right time, blow your fill,
And when there's need, then hold you still,
    And bear your horn, but blow it not.

    I hold him sound, etc.

Whatsoever's in your thought,
Hear it, see it, but say it not;
Then men shall see you are well taught
    To bear your horn, but blow it not.

    I hold him sound, etc.

Of all the riches under the sun,
There never was a better one
Than a man who knows it's truly done
    To bear his horn, but blow it not.

    I hold him sound, etc.

Whatever burns within your breast,
Stop your mouth up with your fist,
And see your first thoughts are your best;
    Then bear your horn, but blow it not.

    I hold him sound, etc.

And when you're sitting with your ale
And singing like a nightingale,
Take care to whom you tell your tale,
    And bear your horn, but blow it not.

    I hold him sound and wisely taught
    Who bears his horn but blows it not.

The Adulterous Falmouth Squire

The sermon-story has a longer history in these islands than the Anglo-Norman lay; which is proof that priestly teachers were not behind secular entertainers in finding ways to hold the attention of the medieval audience. In fact, the short tale with a moral was the preacher's special province. In taking his *exemplum* from any sources of culture available to him – the Bible, classical and post-classical lore, history, or the world around him, and then moralizing upon it, he was using the method hallowed by his faith: the Old Testament writers drew morals from history; Jesus, ideally, from fictions based on the life about him.

The strength of 'The Adulterous Falmouth Squire' as a metrical sermon is that it unashamedly uses a popular metre (Bottom's 'eight and eight') and the secular poet's rhetorical tricks ('I had this story from another', 'Listen, sirs, to what I say', and so forth), and is based avowedly on a true English event. If the retailer of an anecdote can say of the man from whom he heard it, 'Whiche thinge he sayde he dyd se hymselfe,' his moral gains in force from the actuality. For inclusion in the present selection, this late medieval poem has been preferred to others, such as the well-known 'The Dancers of Colbek' from Robert Mannyng of Brunne's 'Handlyng Synne', because, although poorer in poetic skill and formal economy, it is richer in the diversity of its typical medieval elements.

Of these elements, the first is priestly exhortation: in his opening thirteen stanzas, the poet gives us direct advice about our sexual behaviour, threatens us with God's vengeance if we refuse his advice, cites two historical examples and the morals to be drawn from them, and gives us theological glosses upon bastardy, as well as upon beggary in relation to the sacrament of wedlock. At once, launching into narrative, he creates Romance characters of knighthood, and introduces his hero, the child noble of grace and filial in piety. This child, through prayer in his grave-side vigil, gains entrance to the marvellous other-worldly realms of hell and heaven, places which in medieval literature seem always to be easy of access from 'this middle-earth' inhabited by man. Here they are evoked in traditional manner, except that hell is described more economically than is usual, in a single visual flash of ghosts burning under a hill. The description of heaven is more expanded but still brief, a miniature compounded of the New Jerusalem, King Arthur's Camelot, and the Garden of Delight in *Le Roman de la Rose*.

The gruesome pictures of the noble child's father suffering in hell,

> By sinning members high uphung,

and of the blasted tree in paradise, symbolic of human sin, are just indications of the Church's determination to keep the work of the Devil ever before the eyes of its flock, as a fearful warning against error. Perhaps that dark side of the picture is almost balanced by the brightness of the heaven offered by the poet: this place would at once be recognized as the appropriate eternal home for the virtuous among knights and priests. Members of the third and lowliest estate, commoners in the congregation, would naturally aspire to a heaven devised for the two superior estates.

The poem has a Prologue, which purports to be the utterance of the Squire himself, the significantly named Sir William Basterdfeld. His prolix and repetitive harangue is omitted, because its moral point is made both in the poem itself and elsewhere in this book.

43

Turn, O Man, from mischief's snare,
And listen well to my advice:
Of seven deadly sins beware,
And dread the last, the fleshly vice.

For I shall tell you of this last
In terms of truth, no word beyond.
Beware, for God's revenge will blast
The man who breaks his marriage bond!

The sacrament that God first made
Was wedlock, as I tell you true,
So keep it without fear or dread:
It lasts till Day of Doom is due.

If this bond we violate,
And break the word we ought to hold,
Avenging death shall lie in wait
And cast us down to clayey cold.

The greatest king of all the world
For sin may find his crown has gone,
(From old and young this truth I heard)
As Richard[1] did and Solomon.

David, who wrote the Psalter book,
With these bad kings is counted in.
His crown from him Christ Jesus took:
Bathsheba was his cause of sin.

The finest clerk you ever saw
Beneath the arch of heaven's cope
Cannot be priest by holy law
Without a licence from the Pope

If gotten in adultery,
Or if a bastard he is born.
No priestly rank or dignity
Can he possess, that man forlorn.

The beggar at the end of town
Has holy wedlock just as free
As wealthy king and queen in gown –
To all an equal dignity!

If, Man, you knew how foul it were
To take a woman not your wife,
Better by far to suffer here
And quickly die at point of knife;

For if you take another's wife,
You shall beget a wrongful heir,
And so you bring three souls to strife
In hell, to burn and suffer there.

So write these things upon your heart
If you're guilty in this case,
Confessing, doing penance hard.
Bliss is what they hope to embrace,

1. Richard II, 1377–99.

But if in sudden death they die,
Without doing penance after shrift,
They go to hell, without a lie:
No hope of any other shift.

An instance of this I shall tell,
So listen! Thirty years before
The Black Death happened, it befell,
In Falmouth by the western shore,

There dwelt two brothers in the town,
The issue of a father and mother,
And they were squires of great renown –
I had this story from another.

The elder brother had a wife,
The fairest one for miles around,
And yet he led a wicked life –
His soul in bitter chains was bound.

He did not care whose wife he took;
His marriage vows he made in vain,
Till Satan caught him with his crook
And marked him out for fearful pain.

These brothers on the selfsame day
Were killed by enemies in fight:
To hell the elder took his way,
The younger one to heaven bright.

And everywhere this thing was known:
Listen, sirs, to what I say!
Both high and low, yes, everyone,
For love of God, attention, pray!

The elder brother's son, a clerk,
Was then some fifteen years of age,
In soul and sense a lad of mark,
And heir to all the heritage.

In mourning, many a groan he gave,
As children should whose hearts are kind,
And every night beside the grave
He kept his father's soul in mind.

And so he prayed both night and day
To God and to his Mother dear,
To know where now his father lay,
And prayed his spirit might appear.

This noble child, wise and demure,
Stood by his father's grave one eve,
When one in surplice white and pure
Quietly came and plucked his sleeve.

And said to him, 'Child, come with me.
God has listened to your desire.
Child, your father you shall see,
Where he burns in hellish fire.'

He led him up a pleasant slope
And in they went where gaped a hole,
From which was belching fire and smoke,
And ghosts there glowed like burning coal.

He looked on souls in grim despair
Suffering tortures, scorched and stung.
He saw his father burning there,
By sinning members high uphung.

Black devils with their pointed hooks
Ripped his body limb from limb.
'On your father bend your looks.
You wished to see him: speak to him.'

'How is it, Father, in this way
They torture you with torments strong?'
'My son,' he said. 'Alas the day
That ever I did your mother wrong!

'For she was virtuous and fair,
And also trusty, kind, and true.
Alas! What worse than my despair,
My own grim suffering so to brew?'

'Is there, Father, no saint in bliss
Through whom your prayers you used to send,
Who might deliver you from this –
Our Lady Mary, or some friend?'

'Son, all the saints above,' said he,
'And angels under the Trinity
Have no power to rescue me
From all my pain and agony.

'If every blade of grass that grows
Were a priest and prayed for me,
From all these tortures and these woes
Rescued I should never be.

'Yet, you shall be a priest, I feel,
And when you are, for seven years,
At mass or matins, meat or meal,
Never say for me your prayers.

'Listen, son, obey my plea!
For this I warn you well before:
The more you utter prayers for me,
The more my pain shall bind me sore.

'Farewell,' he said, 'my dearest son!
And to the Heavenly Father's troth
I trust you. So bid everyone
Beware of breaking marriage oath.'

The Angel led that father's child
Out of that region woebegone
Into a forest long and wide.
The sun was up, and brightly shone.

He led him to a mansion place:
The gates were crystal, pure in light,
And seemed to him of utmost grace,
And like the beryl, shining bright.

The walls appeared of brilliant gold,
The lofty towers were stout and strong,
And high upon the gates, behold
Minstrelsy and angel song!

The pelican and parrot fair,
The turtle-dove, most sweet and true,
A hundred thousand birds sang there:
The nightingale with melody new.

He saw a tree upon a mound:
The smell of it was harsh and sour;
Pale and wan it was all round,
And it had lost both fruit and flower.

A fearful thing for child to see!
And seeing it, he felt great dread.
'Ah, Lady dear, how can it be
That such a tree should bleed so red?'

The Angel said, 'This is the tree
Whose fruit to Adam God denied:
And therefore driven out was he
To lead his life on earth outside.

'In that same place where fast it bled,
Once grew the apple that Adam bit.
He bit because of what Eve said,
The Devil of hell's work, that was it.

'When any sinner comes herein,
As you behold now here with me,
In vengeance for that wicked sin
The blood comes surging from the tree.'

He led him forth upon a plain,
Where he beheld a fine tent pitched,
And such a tent he'd never seen,
With burnished cloth of gold enriched.

Thereunder sat a creature fair,
As bright as sunbeam undefiled,
And angels did him honour there.
'Behold, this is your uncle, child,'

The Angel said, 'As you can see,
In heaven with endless blisses now.
With him might your father be,
Had he been true to marriage vow.

'His sin has dragged him down to hell,
That everlasting dungeon place,
And there he shall for ever dwell,
Where never comes Redemption's grace.'

Man, to mend your ways begin,
And you shall live secure from woe.
Defend yourself from deadly sin,
And straight to bliss your soul shall go.

Selections from the Bestiary

Nothing can better illustrate the unscientific temper of the medieval mind than the popularity of, and frequent reference to, the Bestiary. The poet of the single surviving Middle English version, which dates from the early thirteenth century, takes thirteen creatures – lion, eagle, adder, ant, stag, fox, spider, whale, mermaid, elephant, turtle-dove, panther, and dove (i.e. pigeon) – outlines wholly fanciful characteristics, and allegorizes this legendary material into improving religious lessons. Many other creatures were the subject of early Christian moralizing fables, and of them all, perhaps three are still alive in idiom: the phoenix, which rises from its own ashes; the pelican, which draws blood from its own breast to feed its young, and is therefore a symbol of Christ; and the ostrich, which buries its head in the sand. The last fiction is still widely believed. Other creatures subjected to Bestiary treatment, and often found in medieval churches, carved in stone or wood, are the tiger, which might be caught by a mirror, being unable to avert its gaze from it; the cockatrice or basilisk, which had the head and wings of a cock and the tail of a serpent, and was hatched by a toad from an egg laid by a seven-year-old cock; the beaver, which was hunted for drugs obtained from its genitals and which, when hard pressed, bit off the prized parts to show that it was no longer worth hunting;[1] the peacock, which was a symbol of immortality; the skiapod, possessor of one enormous foot, which it used as a sunshade when lying on its back; the sawfish, which only chased ships until it was tired, and thus symbolized those who begin well; and the ape, whose ugly behind symbolized devilishness.

The original Bestiary was part of a mystical work in Greek which probably originated in Christian circles in Alexandria during the second century A.D. In a manner owing something to Egyptian

---

1. This story derives from a punning etymology: '*castor*' is Latin for beaver, hence the association with '*castrare*'. But not all medieval scholars were gullible asses; Bartholomew the Englishman writes in the thirteenth century that 'the untruth of the story can be proved any day by looking at beavers'. (See Nikolaus Pevsner: *The Leaves of Southwell*, page 53.)

nature symbolism as well as to Judaic mysticism, it dealt with marvellous qualities of plants and stones as well as beasts, which were then allegorically interpreted along Christian lines, and sheltered under the authority of the Naturalist ('Physiologus'), by whom may have been meant Aristotle. It was translated wherever Christianity went, and the English poet's source appears to have been the Latin-verse Bestiary of an eleventh-century Italian monk named Thetbaldus. The bewildering metrical invention, particularly of the section on the Lion, is however, his own.

44
THE LION

His Nature

The lion, hunter of humans, on hill stands,
Or prowling, picks up prey by scent:
Whichever way he will, he swoops in malice.
Every step he takes, his trail he obliterates,
Dragging tail in the dust in his dire course,
With dust or dew defying his pursuers,
And dashing down to his den to safety.

Innately, by nature too, when newly born,
The lion inert lies, from sleep not stirring,
Until the sun has turned three times about him.

Lastly, the lion, when lying asleep,
Never locks the lids fast when closing his eyes.

Explication

Most high is that hill, the heavenly kingdom:
Our Lord is the lion who lives above there.
When it pleased him to alight below on earth,
The Fiend could never find, though foxy hunter he,
How he drove deep down to the dales of men,
To dwell in his den in that dear Maiden,
Mary, who mothered him for man's benefit.

Our Lord lay dead and still,
And buried was his will;
In tomb of rock he lay
Still till the third day;
His Father helped him then
To rise from death again.

So lived our Lord our life to uphold,
Willingly watchful, like warden of fold:
To us sheep he is shepherd, who shields us from ill,
If we wait on his word, not wandering at will.

45

THE STAG

Two qualities the stag displays:
An explication each conveys.
In a book it is set forth thus
(Men call it 'Physiologus'):

His Nature (1)

He sniffs the adder from its stone,
For under stone the adder goes;
From under stock or under stone,
He sniffs the adder up his nose.
He swiftly swallows it,
And then he burns for it,
Burns with poisoning,
Burns with that baleful thing.
Wisely then, with prudence fleet
He runs, athirst for water sweet,
And avidly he drinks his fill,
Quenching thus his burning ill.
Now is that venom powerless
To do him any wickedness.
Before his cure he casts his horns
In wood or in a brake of thorns:
And that is how this wild deer
Renews his youth: you learn it here.

Explication

Just so, from our forefathers, all
Inherit adders from the Fall
Each time we go against God's word,
By the Snake to evil stirred.
Hence man has a life
Of turmoil and of strife,
Lechery and covetousness,
Wishing harm and greediness,
Pride and overweening:
Such adders are my meaning.
We often burn with passions bad,
And so become just like the mad.
When thus with rage on fire,
We must with keen desire
Run to the living well
Of Christ and so shun hell.
There must we drink God's word
Till all our sins are cured.
There we shall cast aside,
As stag his horns, our pride,
In sight of God our youth restore,
And guard our virtue evermore.

His Nature (2)

Another bent in stags we find,
Which all of us should bear in mind.
They herd in one collective mood,
And when they go in search of food,
And come to water, no one stag
Goes on, and leaves the rest to lag;
But swimming first, a leader goes,
And all the others follow close.
So swimming or wading as they may,
Not one obstructs another's way.
But every creature rests his jaw
On the rump of him who goes before;
And then, if it should so transpire
That the leading stag begin to tire,
The others gather to exhort him,
And helping him, they so support him
That from water to firm ground
They take him quickly, safe and sound.

And so they never fail
Each other on the trail.
Even a hundred of them would
Follow this custom, show this mood.

Explication

This custom we should bear in mind,
And we should leave all sin behind,
And all of us love one another,
And treat each man just like our brother,
And loyally assist each friend
To bear the load which makes him bend:
God shall reward us then
For helping needy men.
We shall have the kingdom of heaven
For services to our fellows given.
No sluggards should we be in following Holy Writ,
For pleasant it is to obey, and great our need of it.

46

THE WHALE

His Nature

The whale's a fish: of all that be,
He's the hugest in the sea.
You could well observe his size
If you saw him with your eyes
Afloat. Indeed, you'd think you saw
An island based on the sea-floor.
This mighty monster of the sea,
When hungry, gapes enormously,
And from his throat his breath is hurled,
The sweetest smell in all the world.
So other fishes towards him go,
Whose scent and taste delight him so,
He savours them in joy awhile:
They have no notion of his guile.
And then the whale shuts his jaw
And sucks those fishes to his maw.
Thus he deceives the fishes small:
The big he cannot hold at all.

The whale lives on the ocean bed
In health and safety, free from dread,
Till summer and winter furiously
Conflicting, storm and stir the sea.
The monster cannot dwell therein
When that season's gales begin,
So turbid is the ocean-floor,
Nor can he bear it any more.
The water thrashes ceaselessly
While that storm is on the sea.
The ships tossed on this tempest high
(Which long to live and hate to die)
Look about them, see the whale,
And thereupon an island hail.
They look on it with great delight,
And pull to it with all their might.
At once they go about to moor,
And everyone proceeds ashore.
They kindle then with steel and stone
A blaze upon this marvellous one:
They warm themselves, and eat and drink:
He feels the fire and makes them sink.
He dives at once to the ocean bed,
And, though unwounded, they are dead.

Explication

Mighty the Devil in strength and in will,
Like witches in witchcraft, doing ill.
With hunger and thirst he makes men a-fire
And burn with many a sinful desire.
His breathing allures, and men come to his face:
Whatever men follow him end in disgrace.
The small fish are those whose faith is unsure.
The big can resist the strength of his lure.
The big, I assert, are those steady and whole,
Whose true faith is perfect in body and soul.

Who listens to the Devil's lore
At last shall find it grieves him sore:
Who hopes by it to prosper well
Shall follow him to darkest hell.

Miscellaneous Secular Poems

The twenty short poems here included are a generous selection from the surviving non-religious poems outside the Harley Lyrics. Professor R. H. Robbins notes the overwhelming preponderance of religious poetry, and gives it as his opinion that it is the temper of the times, and not the destruction of manuscripts containing secular verse, which is responsible for the disproportion. Be that as it may, leaving aside poems by Chaucer and one or two other known poets, and those in the Harley Lyrics, the thirteenth and fourteenth centuries have left us a bare handful of love-lyrics, a few popular ballad-like poems, and a scattering of comic and occasional fragments.

The first two poems, nos. 47 and 48, are well known. They are minstrel scraps which survive because they were scribbled on the fly-leaf of a religious work of the early fourteenth century. The next two pieces, nos. 49 and 50, survive from the same manuscript, but are less well known. It is tempting to associate with no. 50 the quatrain, no. 51, which Professor Robbins found on a different manuscript, but quotes in his note on 'All night by the rose'.

'Tell me, broom wizard' (no. 52) is a fascinating folk poem which Carleton Brown found quoted in an early thirteenth-century sermon example. While the advice to women to talk less is found wherever literature is created by men, its setting here calls for comment. The advice of soothsayers could be had in the towns, but if stronger magic than theirs was required, the inquirer had to go to the wild wood. In this sense, 'broom' may be used as a synonym for 'heath', the place where dark wisdom might be tapped, but also where illicit lovers might be undisturbed. Then the magical properties of the plant broom must be considered: in 'The Broomfield Wager', a folk-song found in Somerset by Cecil Sharp, a girl who is afraid of losing her virginity 'is instructed by a witch how to keep her lover asleep by means of the magical properties of broom flowers, whose perfume was supposed to be a narcotic' (James Reeves, *The Idiom of the People*, page 94). Broom gave power of all kinds, including sexual power: witches rode upon it, and in some cultures, broom outside the door repelled death. It is also, in plant lore, the symbol of humility; which made Geoffrey of Anjou, the founder of the Plantagenets (=*planta genista*), assume it as emblem when making pilgrimage to the Holy Land. At least two of these characteristics illuminate its presence in our little poem.

Poem no. 53 is a *chanson d'aventure* from the first decade of the fourteenth century. In this type of poem, the hero is always a knightly rider who has an encounter. In a parallel poem in French, there is a fourth stanza recording the girl's acceptance of the rider in place of the faithless wooer – a sudden yielding which is often found at the end of such poems (see no. 92).

Poem no. 54 is a full working of a favourite motif, the definition of love, and is interesting for the indication it gives of an early approximation to standard ballad metre. The three love lyrics which follow (nos. 55-7) are from the famous minstrel manuscript Sloane 2593. Although they needed slight adjustment rather than translation, no anthology of medieval poetry could be complete without them. They reflect, in both their courtly and popular aspects, the light and grace which became apparent before love-poetry plunged into the wastes of the aureate convention of the fifteenth century. The series of riddles in poem no. 56 is also found in a folk-song, in which a Captain Wedderburn, set them by his haughty lover, solves them and so wins her: the cherry is a tree of Venus; the dove is, of course, that goddess's bird, but the briar, unlike all other roses, which are flowers of Venus, comes under Jupiter. In *The Oxford Dictionary of Nursery Rhymes* there is a discussion of the poem on page 387, and it is suggested that it was already old when the minstrel wrote it down.

Nos. 58 and 59 are late medieval carols on a theme fertile in all ages – the pregnancy lament. The first gains distinction from the realism of domestic description and the charming innuendo of the third stanza, and the second is a humorous comment on the concupiscence of clerics, one of the abuses constantly attacked by the mendicant orders.

Poem no. 60 is a reminder of what the average teacher was, and of the attitude to him of his students. When a Master of Arts took his degree, he was given a rod of birch, which he was expected to use on his pupils. There is a record of an Oxford schoolmaster being drowned in a mill pond in 1301, while climbing a willow tree to replenish his stock of canes.[1] In such a case, it was always possible that the pupils were responsible; the writer of our poem seems capable of such an act.

The alliterative curiosity about blacksmiths (no. 61) is well known, but is not nearly as curious as the poem about the Man in the Moon (no. 62), which has been placed here among the oddities, although it is from the Harley Lyrics manuscript. The idea of there being a Man in the Moon derives from the dark patches, which are assumed to be all sorts of things in various cultures. Possibly some conscious Christianizing of old myth is responsible for the association of the Man in the Moon with Cain, who is carrying the thorns which symbolize the Fall, and is accompanied by the Devil in canine shape. Sometimes he is another sinner, Judas. But probably, in our poem, he is the man mentioned in Numbers xv, 32–36, who was stoned to death, as the Law required, for gathering sticks on the sabbath. He is linked in the popular mind with that hapless contemporary, the poor gatherer of fuel on rich men's land. If law and order can be thwarted by a happy conspiracy of underdogs. . . . The last line but two refers to the gradual disappearance of the 'Man' as the moon wanes.

The fashion satire (no. 63), which is from the same source, offers the view that items of the latest vogue are in order only if the whole feminine ensemble is in accord, and worn by a noblewoman; and that such vanities betoken immorality. The rumbustiousness of the writing is of a kind which marks the political poems of the period.

The nonsense miniatures on the lion, bear, and dragon (nos. 64–66) seem to have been written by some Belgian Hare or Ogden Nash of the late fourteenth century. It is strange that dragons, so fearsome in Anglo-Saxon literature, figure less in the Anglo-Norman consciousness than in the Gothic period. Then they appear plentifully in cathedral sculpture (there are some long-eared ones in Exeter Cathedral) and become absorbed in the Bestiary tradition. The dragon is the only beast which is not attracted by the sweet breath of the panther, and so becomes a symbol of all those who reject Christ.

---

1. Quoted by W. O. Hassall in *How They Lived*, page 241.

47

I am from Ireland,
And from the holy land
    Of Ireland.
Good sir, I beg of you,
For holy charity,
Come and dance with me
    In Ireland.

48

Maiden on the moor lay,
On the moor lay,
Seven nights full and a day.
Maiden on the moor lay,
On the moor lay,
Seven nights full and a day.

Well was her meat:
What was her meat?
The primrose and the –
The primrose and the –
Well was her meat:
The primrose and the violet.[1]

Well was her drink:
What was her drink?
The chilled water of the –
The chilled water of the –
Well was her drink:
What was her drink?
The chilled water of the well-spring.

Well was her bower:
What was her bower?
The red rose and the –
The red rose and the –
Well was her bower:
What was her bower?
The red rose and the lily flower.

1. The primrose and the violet are flowers of Venus, as well as the rose. All four flowers mentioned are medicinal herbs.

49[1]

Of every kind of tree,
Of every kind of tree,
The hawthorn blows the sweetest
Of every kind of tree.

My lover she shall be,
My lover she shall be
Of earthly girls the fairest,
My lover she shall be.

50

All night by the rose, rose,
All night by the rose I lay;
I dared not steal the rose-tree,
But I bore the flower away.

51

I am Rose, alas for me,
Though sweeter than the sweet I be;
I grow in pain and misery,
For hand of churl has done for me.

52

'Tell me, broom wizard, tell me,
Teach me what to do,
To make my husband love me:
Tell me, broom wizard, do!'

'Silent tongue and still
Shall bring you all your will.'

1. Hawthorn is 'the symbol of good hope in the language of flowers, because it shows that winter is over and spring is at hand', states Brewer in his *Dictionary of Phrase and Fable*. In Athens, the marriage-torch was made of hawthorn.

53[1]

'Now blossoms the spray:
All for love I am so sick,
My sleep has gone away.'

On horseback as I rode one day
    Adventuring,
I chanced to hear while on my way
    A maiden sing:
    'Clod to him cling!
Alas to love in suffering
    My life away!'
        'Now blossoms the spray, etc.'

And hearing that delightful tune,
    I went to see;
And in a glade I found her soon
    In ecstasy
    Beneath a tree.
I asked, 'Why sing so ceaselessly,
    O maiden gay?'
        'Now blossoms the spray, etc.'

And then replied that lovely she,
    (Her words were few)
'My lover swore on oath to me
    His love was true:
    He's changed for new.
May it bring him grief and rue
    This very day!
        Now blossoms the spray:
        All for love I am so sick,
        My sleep has gone away.'

1. In a letter of 1944 to Josef Szigeti, quoted in the *London Magazine* of July 1963, Béla Bartók, at work on Wallachian folk-song, writes, 'To be jilted, abandoned, is a bigger *malheur* for the girl than for the lad. . . . Girls (or women) are so much more vehement, full of fury than the men. . . . There are ever so many more cursing texts about girls vilifying faithless men than vice versa' – which illuminates an entire human landscape, of which our poem is a part.

54

Love is soft and love is sweet, and speaks in accents fair;
Love is mighty agony, and love is mighty care;
Love is utmost ecstasy and love is keen to dare:
Love is wretched misery; to live with, it's despair.

Love's a lottery, mars your luck or gives you pleasures gay;
Love is lecherous, love is loose, and likely to betray;
Love's a tyrant here on earth, not easy to gainsay;
Love throughout this land of ours sends faithful ones astray.

Love's a stern and valiant knight, strong astride a steed;
Love's a thing that pleasures every longing woman's need;
Love persists and keeps its heat like any glowing gleed;[1]
Love puts girls in floods of tears, they rage and cry indeed.

Love maintains his bailiwick in every path and street;
Love can wet with tears the cheek of any maiden sweet;
Love by chance brings misery inflamed with fever heat;
Love is wise and love is wary, wants its way complete.

Love's the softest, sweetest thing that in the heart may sleep;
Love is craft, and for its woes is well equipped to weep;
Love is false and love is eager, forces folk to long;
Love is foolish, love is firm, and love is comfort strong:
Love's a marvel to the man who treats of it in song.

Love is weal and love is woe, in gladness can maintain us;
Love is life and love is death, and love can well sustain us.

If love had strength for suffering as first it has when keen,
Then love would be the worthiest thing the world had ever seen;
But this is what is sung of it, and so it's ever been:
'Love begins in mighty pain and ends in grief and spleen,
With noble lady, steady wife, with virgin or with queen!'

55

I newly have a garden
Which newly is begun:
I know not such a garden
Beneath the sun.

1. Gleed = coal.

I've a pear-tree[1] in the middle
Of my garden there:
Mature fruit it grows not,
But early Jennet-pear.

The prettiest girl in our town
Begged a boon of me:
To graft for her a scion
From my pear-tree.

When I'd done the grafting
Entirely to her pleasure,
With wine and ale she plied me
In fullest measure.

This scion I had grafted
Right up in her home,
And twenty weeks later
It quickened in her womb.

I met that pretty maiden
After just a year:
She said it was a Robert –,
No early Jennet-pear!

56

I have a little sister
Far beyond the sea,
And many love-tokens
Has she sent me.

She sent me a cherry
Without any stone;
She sent me a dove
Without any bone;

She sent me a briar
Without branch or leaf;
She bade me love my lover
Without any grief.

1. The pear-tree is a tree of Venus. Compare the pear-tree joke, in Chaucer's
The Merchant's Tale.

How can there be a cherry
Without any stone?
How can there be a dove
Without any bone?

How can there be a briar
Without branch or leaf?
How can I love my lover
Without any grief?

When the cherry was a blossom,
It had no stone;
When the dove was an egg,
It had no bone;

When the briar was a seed,
It lacked branch and leaf;
So having what she loves,
A girl's without grief.

57

I have a noble cockerel
Whose crowing starts my day:
He makes me get up early
My morning prayer to say.

I have a noble cockerel
Of lofty pedigree:
His comb is of red coral,
His tail jet-black to see.

I have a noble cockerel;
He comes of gentle kind:
His comb is of red coral,
His tail is of Ind.

His legs are all of azure,
Graceful, soft, and slim:
His spurs are silver white
Deep to the root of him.

His eyes are of crystal,
Sweetly set in amber;
And every night he perches
In my lady's chamber.

58

The Servant Girl's Holiday

I've waited longing for today:
Spindle, bobbin, and spool, away!
In joy and bliss I'm off to play
 Upon this high holiday.

 Spindle, bobbin, and spool, away,
 For joy that it's a holiday!

The dirt upon the floor's unswept,
The fireplace isn't cleaned and kept,
I haven't cut the rushes yet
 Upon this high holiday.

 Spindle, bobbin, etc.

The cooking herbs I must fetch in,
And fix my kerchief under my chin.
Darling Jack, lend me a pin
 To fix me well this holiday!

 Spindle, bobbin, etc.

Now midday has almost come,
And all my chores are still not done:
I'll clean my shoes till they become
 Bright for a high holiday.

 Spindle, bobbin, etc.

In pails the milk has got to go;
I ought to spread this bowl of dough –
It clogs my nails and fingers so
 As I knead this holiday!

 Spindle, bobbin, etc.

Jack will take me on my way,
And with me he will want to play:
I needn't fear my lady's nay
 On such a high holiday!

 Spindle, bobbin, etc.

And when we stop beside the track
At the inn this Sunday, Jack
Will wet my whistle and pay my whack
   As on every holiday.

   Spindle, bobbin, etc.

Then he'll take me by the hand
And lay me down upon the land
And make my buttocks feel like sand
   Upon this high holiday.

   Spindle, bobbin, etc.

In he'll push and out he'll go,
With me beneath him lying low:
'By God's death, you do me woe
   Upon this high holiday!'

   Spindle, bobbin, etc.

Soon my belly began to swell
As round and great as any bell;
And to my dame I dared not tell
   What happened to me that holiday.

   Spindle, bobbin, and spool, away,
   For joy that it's a holiday!

59

Not long ago I met a clerk,
And he went craftily to work;
His subtle talk he bade me mark,
And secretly to weigh of it.

   Ah dear God, I am forsaken,
      Now my maidenhead is taken!

It seems he had a magic skill,
And this is why I think so still:
Because when he declared his will,
I could not say him nay of it.

   Ah dear God, etc.

When he and I got under sheet,
I let him have his way complete,
And now my girdle will not meet.
Dear God, what shall I say of it?

   Ah dear God, etc.

I shall say to man and page
That I have been on pilgrimage.
If priest again show lustful rage,
I'll not let him make play of it.

Ah dear God, I am forsaken,
Now my maidenhead is taken!

60

Brainy teacher, is it your
Desire to beat us daily more,
Like a blooming lord?
We'd rather leave your school for good,
And learn another livelihood
Than jump to your bossy word.

But if we caught you, with God's will,
At the stones beside the mill,
Or by the crab-apple tree,
We'd scar you once upon your skin
For every swishing: then your kin
Would give you sympathy.

And if the Devil – he's your Puck –
Waved his claw to bring you luck,
You'd get it then worse still.
If he prayed one word for you,
We'd knock him down and belt him too,
Not spare you at his will.

For many times we groan and sigh
When signals from his glinting eye
Make you beat our backs;
For you and he are of one mind,
And daily you are close combined
To give us mighty whacks.

61

Swarthy smoke-blackened smiths, smudged with soot,
Drive me to death with the din of their banging.
Men never knew such a noise at night!
Such clattering and clanging, such clamour of scoundrels!
Crabbed and crooked, they cry, 'Coal! Coal!'
And blow with their bellows till their brains burst.

'Huff! Puff!' pants one: 'Haff! Paff!' another.
They spit and they sprawl and they spin many yarns.
They grate and grind their teeth, and groan together,
Hot with the heaving of their hard hammers.
Aprons they have, of hide of the bull,
And greaves as leg-guards against glowing sparks.
Heavy hammers they have, and hit hard with them;
Sturdy strokes they strike on their steel anvils.
Lus, bus! Las, bas! they beat in turn –
Such a doleful din, may the Devil destroy it!
The smith stretches a scrap, strikes a smaller,
Twines the two together, and tinkles a treble note:
Tik, tak! Hic, hac! Tiket, taket! Tyk, tak!
Bus, lus! Bas, las! Such a life they lead,
These Dobbin-dressers: Christ doom them to misery!
There's no rest at night for the noise of their water-fizzing.[1]

62

The Man in the Moon can stand or stride,
    And on a forked stick a bundle he bears.
Much wonder it is that he doesn't slip-slide;
    For fear of a fall he shudders and veers.
By the freezing of frost he is heavily tried.
    His clothing gets ripped when his thorn-faggot tears,
And only that burden of thorn can decide
    When he bends down and sits, or what clothing he wears.

What route do you think that the weird chap takes?
    One foot is behind and the other before,
But he moves not a yard for the effort he makes –
    Such a slow-moving fellow the earth never saw!
He's out in the field and fiddling with stakes,
    And wants to find thorns to strengthen his door:
The day will be lost if his double-edged axe
    Won't chop him a load to bundle and store.

Wherever he is, on high or much higher,
    Alive on the moon, and born there and bred,
He leans on his fork like a weary grey friar,
    A crooked old idler half crippled with dread.

    1. i.e. the noise of hot iron being plunged into water.

It's long since we saw him, and if you inquire,
    You'll find that his searching for thorns hasn't sped:
The bailiff has spotted him hacking down briar,
    And taken a pledge that'll bother his head.

Your pledge may be taken, but bring home your boughs:
    Put your other foot forward and stride out free:
We'll play host to the bailiff here in the house,
    And make him at ease in the highest degree.
We'll give him strong drink till his spirits rouse;
    Our housewife will pleasantly sit on his knee,
And when he's as drunk as a drowning mouse,
    We'll take back the pledge from the bailiff, you'll see.

The fellow won't listen, though loudly I cry.
    I reckon he's deaf: Devil tear him, I say!
In spite of my bellows, he just won't try.
    He hasn't a clue about justice's way.
Hi! Hubert, you stockinged old magpie, hi!
    There's a gorge busy gobbling you! Get clear away!
My teeth grind with rage as I get no reply,
    And the chap won't show up before dawn of the day.

63[1]

Lord who grants us life and looks upon us all,
You need not fight with knife in filthy human brawl!
But man and maid and wife are stiff with fright and awe,
Lest you be stern in strife, bearing Eden's law
            In mind,
        That all mankind
Should live in joy and love, and leave all sin behind.

Pride now takes the prize whenever people play:
Of many women unwise, I say my warning say,
For if a lady nice is dressed in noble array,
Then every whore there is will hop the selfsame way.
            In pride
        The shrouded shrew will stride
Although she hasn't a smock her ugly arse to hide.

1. 'Bose': padding to give protuberant effect in dress. 'Caul': container for plaits, once at back of head, but for a long time at both temples, framing the face. 'Bout', 'barbette': parts of the head-dress. 'Fillet': either simple headband, or pillbox-shaped hat. 'Jewels': M.E. 'locket', probably the jewelled working on the caul.

The bose to castle came to beautify the fair.
It brought those beauties fame, and that is why it's there;
But giddy girls of the game groan if they can't get it.
The cost these frills shall claim when harlots so coquette it!
        In hell
        With devils they shall dwell
Because of cauls that clog and cleave to cheeks that swell.

They've plenty of padding fine: the bose these bitches bear.
They sit like hunted swine, with ears all sunk for care.
The lists of love's new line, which any wench can wear!
All comes to sad decline in those trollop-trappings there.
        For these
        The Devil sits at ease
On judge's throne in hell, rejecting all their pleas.

Though jewels may be set beside her other eye,
They shall with worse be wet, being open to the sky.
The bout and the barbette must with the band comply;
If false the fillet set, she'll hold her head up high
        To show
        What all may see and know:
That she's a whore among the lowest of the low.

64

The Lion

The Lion is wonderfully strong
   And full of wicked skill;
     And whether he play
     Or seize his prey,
   He cannot choose but kill.

65

The Bear

Beware of the Bear lest by chance he bite:
He rarely stops play but to bite or to smite.

66

The Dragon

I shall swallow you humans regardless, the lot —
Yet some I might spare: others, not.

Political Poems

Of the three poems included, the first two, which date from 1265 and about 1334, are puffed with savage gibe and pitiless partisanship, and are more interesting as social documents than as poetry, although both writers adorn their fulminations with the metrical elaborations proper to true poets of their times. The Provençal name for this kind of poem, a satirical form of the courtly lyric which lashed political and other enemies, is the *sirventes*.

Poem no. 67, which is from the Harley Lyrics manuscript, is concerned with the Battle of Lewes, 1264, in which the Barons defeated Henry III and his brother Richard. Richard, the villain of the poem, was the only Englishman ever to rule the Holy Roman Empire, but his hold on it was precarious, and although crowned at Aachen, he was never formally recognized by the Pope. The particular bitterness against him which the Barons' poet shows was due to Richard's having shifted, during the long struggles of Henry III's reign, his allegiance from the Barons to the court. When he became an unwavering supporter of his brother, he further alienated sympathy by his exactions as regent when Henry was fighting in Ireland, and his enlistment of financial support from the Jews, the creditors of many nobles. Though personally ambitious, Richard appears to have been a tireless negotiator who on the whole preferred buying his way forward to fighting. In order to understand the poem, the reader needs to know the following:

Richard had come to England to raise funds for the ruling of his continental empire (stanza one). His activities as regent are referred to; Wallingford was his own estate, and his castle there was his first prison after Lewes (stanza two). During the battle, Richard became separated from his brother, and retreated to a mill, which he attempted to fortify (stanza three). Most of Richard's soldiers were from the Continent (stanza four). The Earl of Warynne and Sir Hugh de Bigot were partisans of the King, and are listed among a group who fled from the field, being daunted by 'the ferocity of the Barons'; Simon de Montfort was the leader of the Barons, and son of the political opportunist who led the crusade against the Albigensians (see page 22) (stanzas five to seven). Edward, later Edward I, was the King's son, who was imprisoned in Dover Castle some time after the battle (stanza eight). Simon de Montfort, who was godfather to Prince Edward as well as uncle, was killed in the following year at the Battle of Evesham, which settled the royal supremacy over the Barons for the time being. Simon was a pious and learned man of great popular reputation, and an excellent general. After his death he was regarded as something of a saint, and his name was often coupled with that of Thomas à Becket. His old enemy, Richard, showed mercy and even kindness to Simon the Younger after Evesham.

We have the name, but no other knowledge, of the poet of no. 68 – Laurence Minot, the writer of several songs celebrating the triumphs of Edward III. He is the first writer to strike the patriotic note; whether the enemy is French or Scottish, there is no division within the English camp. He works a new feeling in the old mould: stock alliterative phrases, thundering rhymes and link words marshal the ancient savagery to the strange purposes of national unity. Although the poet introduces his work as a song upon Bannockburn, the poem is in fact the second of two on the much later battle of Halidon Hill (1333), which was apparently regarded as ample English revenge for the defeat of nineteen years before. While besieging Berwick, Edward III was attacked by a Scottish force much bigger than his own, but with the sea, the Tweed, and the hostile Berwick garrison preventing any retreat, he used his hill position to achieve a triumphant victory against odds. The 'St John's town' of the poem is Perth, which was occupied by the English, and Bruges was a Scottish rallying point on the Continent. Apart from guile, which is standard for enemies, the Scottish characteristics mentioned are the makeshift footwear ('brogues'), made of raw hide with the hairy surface outwards, and the habit of moving about with a small bag containing all belongings, which spared Scottish armies the encumbrance of the baggage-train. It was such marks of simplicity that led Higden, the contemporary writer of improving chronicles, to say of the Scots, 'By mixing with Englishmen they be much amended' (quoted by G. G. Coulton, *Medieval Panorama*, page 66).

'On the Death of Edward III' is a poem full of misgiving about the future of England towards the end of the fourteenth century. The

'Duke Henry' of stanza nine had died of the plague in 1361, the
Black Prince in 1376, and Edward III, the old victor of so many wars,
in 1377; and to replace these tried leaders there was only the young
Richard II, the 'sprig' of stanza twelve. The old chauvinistic fury is
still there, but the revenges of time, plague and the nation's enemies
have brought in an elegiac note which commends the work as a poem,
in spite of the conventional rhetoric about the ship of state.

67

Song of the Battle of Lewes, 1264

Now sit you all still and listen to me!
By my faith, the Emperor of Germany
Asked thirty thousand pounds, that did he,
To settle the peace that side of the sea,
    And more he raked in, sir!

Dick, up to every treacherous trick,
    Your crafty career's done in, sir!

Richard of Germany, while he was king,
On fornication spent everything:
All Wallingford hasn't a farthing to bring.
Let him draw as he brews, drink suffering,
    In spite of Windsor![1]

Dick, etc.

The Emperor of Germany thought he'd done well
To make a strong fortress out of a mill.
His swords were so sharp his defence would excel,
And he thought each mill-sail a mangonel[2]
    To help Windsor.

Dick, etc.

The Emperor of Germany gathered his host,
And made a redoubt of a miller's post;
All puffed up with pride and bursting with boast,
He'd brought from Germany many a sad ghost
    To strengthen Windsor.

Dick, etc.

    1. i.e. Henry III.
    2. A battle-engine for slinging.

By the God that's above us, much did he sin
To let slip abroad the Earl of Warynne,
Who plundered all England, from mountain to fen,
Of silver and gold, and went off with it then
      For love of Windsor.

Dick, etc.

Sir Simon de Montfort took oath by his chin
That if he laid hands on the Earl of Warynne,
That earl nevermore should see castle or kin,
Or with sword or buckler or sharp javelin
      Help Windsor.

Dick, etc.

By his head Sir Simon de Montfort swore
That if he had Sir Hugh de Bigot once more,
Although he paid tribute, a twelvemonth's score,
He'd never again put his foot to the floor
      To help Windsor.

Dick, etc.

Sir Edward, whether you like it or not,
With you riding spurless, your grey shall trot
The straight road to Dover, not turning one jot;
You'll nevermore battle or sally with shot:
      Your grief has come in, sir!

For your uncle's advice, in your scoundrelly clique,
      You gave not a pin, sir!

Dick, up to every treacherous trick,
      Your crafty career's done in, sir!

68

The Battle of Bannockburn

BY LAURENCE MINOT

Attend my tale, and you shall learn
About the Battle of Bannockburn.

Scots from Berwick and Aberdeen,
At Bannockburn so fierce and keen,
You killed the innocent, as was seen;
But now King Edward's avenged it clean:
      Avenged it clean, and well worth while.
      But watch the Scots, they're full of guile.

Where are you Scots of St John's town?
Your banner's boast is beaten down;
Sir Edward's ready for your bragged renown:
He'll kindle your care and crack your crown.
    He cracked your crown, and well worth while:
    Shame on the Scots, they're full of guile!

The Scots of Stirling were stern and proud;
Nor God nor good men had them cowed.
The robbers, they raided round about,
But in the end Edward put them to rout.
    He put them to rout, and well worth while:
    They'll always lose, though full of guile.

You clumping brogue, now kindles your care!
You boasting bagman, your bothy's bare!
You wily traitor, where now? Where?
Go back to Bruges, and bed down there!
    Yes, there, and waste a weary while!
    Your Dundee dwelling's down through your guile.

The Scot goes to Bruges and strolls the streets;
He plans for England heavy defeats;
He promptly complains to people he greets,
But few to cure his cares he meets.
    Few cure his cares, and well worth while:
    He threatens with traitors' tricks and guile.

But many threaten and utter ill
Who were better silent, standing stone-still.
The Scot has wind and spare to spill,
But in the end Edward shall have his will.
    He had his will at Berwick, and well worth while:
    Scots gave up the keys: yet guard against their guile!

69

On the Death of Edward III

Ah dear God, how can it be
    That all things waste and wear away?
Friendship is but vanity,
    And barely lasts the length of day.
    When put to proof, men go astray.
Averse to loss, to gain inclined:
    So fickle is their faith, I say,
That out of sight is out of mind.

Yes, not without a cause I speak,
 And therefore you should take good heed,
For if my meaning you would seek,
 I shall tell you truth indeed,
 And then for shame your hearts will bleed
If to wisdom you're inclined.
 He who was our utmost speed
Is out of sight and out of mind.

Some time an English ship we had:
 Noble it was, and high of tower,
And held through Christendom in dread.
 It bravely bore its battle hour,
 Most stoutly stood the sea-squall's power
And other storms of every kind.
 Yet now that ship, which bore the flower,
Is out of sight and out of mind.

In that ship there was a rudder,
 Which steered the ship and governed it.
The world will not see such another,
 It seems to me in sense and wit.
 While ship and rudder were surely knit,
They feared no storm of wave or wind:
 But now asunder they are split,
And out of sight is out of mind.

All seas that ship has seen and sailed,
 Adventuring in bold career;
For wind or weather it never failed
 While that rudder lasted here.
 And come a calm or storm severe,
Safe harbour-home that ship would find.
 Now is that ship, I speak out clear,
Both out of sight and out of mind.

I liken this good ship I saw
 To the chivalry of this land,
Who once gave nothing, not a straw,
 For all of France, I understand.
 They caught and killed them with the hand,
The powers of France, of every kind;
 Enslaved the king at their command:
But now all that is out of mind.

That ship possessed a stout-based mast,
    A sail besides both strong and large,
Which made that good ship never aghast
    To take a mighty matter in charge.
    And to that ship belonged a barge
Which counted France a puff of wind.
    To us it was a shielding targe,
But now it's wholly out of mind.

The rudder was not oak or elm,
    But Edward the Third, noble Knight.
The Prince his son, who manned the helm,
    Was never defeated in the fight.
    The King he rode and sailed aright;
The Prince no fear could ever find:
    But now our thoughts of them are slight,
For out of sight is out of mind.

Duke Henry was that speedy barge,
    A noble knight in the battle-throe,
Who in his allegiance large
    Bore many a bitter, furious blow.
    When bounds were broken by the foe,
A way to scourge them he would find.
    But now that lord is laid full low;
And out of sight is out of mind.

The Commons, by the cross on high,
    I liken to the vessel's mast,
Who with their wealth and property
    Maintained the war from first to last.
    That ship was blown along with blast
Of goodly prayers, its guiding wind.
    Devotion now away is cast:
Good deeds have gone clean out of mind.

And so these lords are laid full low.
    The stock that stems has the self-same root:
A sprig is thrusting, starts to grow,
    Who shall, I hope, to us bring good,
    And keep his foemen underfoot,
And be enthroned as kingly kind.
    May Christ so grant that this young shoot,
Though out of sight, be kept in mind!

When this sprig's to stature grown,
 And strong and sturdy, tough and trim,
I pray he may be proudly known,
 Of many lands the conqueror grim,
 For he is fit in heart and limb
To strive and sweat in the battle-grind.
 Christ grant that we so fare with him
That out of sight be ever in mind!

So let me urge what I have said.
 Until this sprig have time to grow,
Let every man hold up his head
 To serve him, both the high and low.
— The French know how to boast and blow,
When threats and gibes for us they find;
 And we're unnatural, sluggish, slow,
When out of sight is out of mind.

So may your thoughts, good sirs, be one
 With our doughty king who died when old,
And with Prince Edward too, his son,
 True fountain of the spirit bold.
 I know not when we shall behold
Two lords of such a lofty kind.
 Yet now their fame is hardly told:
It's out of sight and out of mind.

Patience

Soon after the middle of the fourteenth century, a north-western contemporary of Chaucer's, whose name has not survived on the single manuscript of the poem, composed the minor epic, 'Patience'. The four narrative poems on this manuscript, which lack titles, are generally known as 'Pearl', 'Cleanness' or 'Purity', 'Patience', and *Sir Gawain and the Green Knight*, and are thought to be by the same author. Gollancz surmises that 'Patience' was written in about 1360; Bateson, citing parallels with the B-text of *Piers Plowman*, in about 1377.

'Cleanness' and 'Patience' appear to be companion pieces. 'Cleanness' recommends the virtue of its title by relating the stories of The Flood, Sodom and Gomorrah, and Balshazzar's Feast: 'Patience' is also concerned with its single virtue, as it is exemplified by the story of Jonah and the Whale. However, if Jonah's shortcoming is reckoned to be the opposite of the virtue advocated by the poet-homilist, perhaps the poem should be entitled 'Forbearance', for that seems to be the exact quality demonstrated by Jonah's God.

Like more than one other medieval homilist, the poet sets his work in motion by reviewing the Beatitudes, although none of the qualities there blessed may, in the strictest sense, be called 'Patience', which is rather a quality underlying the line

Happy are they also whose hearts are well governed.

He then proceeds to identify his own lot with that of Jonah, and to reflect on Jonah's failure to adopt an orthodox, Augustinian acceptance of his predestined lot. This prologue, like the beginnings of the four sections of the poem, which roughly correspond to the chapter divisions in the Vulgate, is headed on the manuscript with a coloured capital initial letter.

The long tradition of the English sermon has been upheld by many preachers with fine narrative and descriptive gifts, and the best of them have subordinated their poetic skill to their didactic aim. So it is with the poet of 'Patience', who fixes the minds of his audience on the Beatitudes, and never allows them to forget his purpose thereafter. But the divine maxims and judgements in the poem come from the mouth of a God dramatically realized as a person, and the hasty moralizings, genuine repentance, and final disillusion of Jonah help to create a character who is organic in his own right as well as being a faithful and inspired extension of the Bible figure. The poet, in fact, is as good as the best medieval dramatists at bringing his Bible story to life by vivid characterization and furious action.

It seems to be the custom to single out for praise the vigorous description of the storm at sea, with much the same impulse as once drove anthologists to abstract the 'famous speeches' from Shakespeare's plays; but it is a bad custom, if indeed it is still followed. The poet's main achievement in 'Patience' is to make a harmonious artefact of his lofty moral vision; so that the grim gusto of the description of the belly of the whale, and the abasing vehemence of Jonah's prayer and repentance inside the monster, which follows, each gain by the juxtaposition. Even in his imagery, the poet remembers: Jonah is thrown down the throat of the whale (into 'the guts of hell'!)

> as a thing no more compressed
> Than mote entering minster door, so mighty its gullet

— a gracefully illuminating paradox. His nice sense of irony often shows through such parallelisms, as when Jonah, having found a corner in the belly of the whale free from filth and defilement,

> Sat as safe and sound, except for the gloom,
> As in the bowels of the boat, where he had been asleep before.

Many people tend to forget what happens to Jonah after he is spewed out by the whale; they only remember that Nineveh is not destroyed, and that Jonah is accordingly confounded. After reading this poem, they will be unlikely to forget the proper end of the tale. For God there demonstrates to Jonah that the removal of even a small and recently acquired comfort can bring hardship. The graphic description of Jonah

> So content with his trusty gourd, tumbling about beneath it,
> That devil of a bit for his diet that day cared he,

followed by his intemperate outburst at the withering of the creeper, bring the lesson of the Book of Jonah into precise focus: God, by his own action, recommends forbearance to Man.

But for all his moral earnestness, the poet rides our consciences lightly. At the end, struck as we are by the brilliance of the action and the manifest forbearance of God, we find the poet content to point only a four-line moral; and to apply it to himself at that.

'Patience' is written in the late medieval form of Old English alliterative verse, which the translation maintains. The lines seem to be grouped in fours, but not consistently throughout; and the poem is nearer to the Old English tradition in language and mood than the other poems attributed to the author.

It is strange that the group of magnificent poems of which 'Patience' is one should have lain in manuscript, apparently unknown, and hence without influence on the main stream of our literature, from the Middle Ages until the nineteenth century.

70

PATIENCE

or, Jonah and the Whale

Patience is a princely thing, though displeasing often.
When heavy hearts are scorned, or otherwise hurt,
Sufferance may assuage and soothe the searing pain:
It subdues dire evil and does away with malice.

For when a man bears woe, he wins joy later,
But, fretting at misfortune, he feels it more forcefully:
So better it is to bear the blow in due time
Than express my impatience, in spite of the pain.

I heard one holy day in the high mass
From Matthew, what the Master taught to his men:
Eight beatitudes, each with its reward
By its separate deserving, he spoke to them of.

Happy are they whose hearts are humbly poor;
They shall have the heavenly kingdom for ever.
Happy are they also who behave meekly;
They shall have the whole earth and all that they wish.

Happy are they also whose anguish makes them weep;
For comfort shall come to them in many countries.
Happy are they also who hunger for righteousness;
For they shall freely be filled full of good things.

Happy are they also whose hearts are pitiful;
For all manner of mercy shall make their reward.
Happy are they also whose hearts are pure;
In full sight shall they see the Saviour enthroned.

Happy are they also who hold to peace;
For they shall be styled the sons of God.
Happy are they also whose hearts are well governed;
As I said earlier, heaven shall be theirs.

These are all the eight beatitudes taught us:
Let us love these ladies in likeness of virtues —
Lady Poverty, Lady Pity, Lady Penance the third,
Lady Meekness, Lady Mercy, immaculate Purity,

Lady Peace, and Lady Patience placed at the end.
Happy he who had one, though all were better!
Yet though Poverty is the pith of my present problem,
I shall put forward Patience, and take pleasure in both.

For the text there twins these two in its theme,
Fitting them in one form, first and last in order,
Weighing their wisdom with rewards alike:
Besides, I assert they are of similar kind.

For Poverty's presence is proof against all,
And she dwells wherever she will, willy-nilly,
Oppressing till pain appears to man,
Who is bound to bear it, though boldly he object.

Thus Poverty and Patience are plainly play-fellows.
Since I am saddled with them, and suffer I must,
It is less painful to approve them, and praise their appearance,
Than be hostile and hate them, and have things worse.

If I am due for my destiny, and addressed to receive it,
Does slighting or scorning it serve my cause?
If my liege lord[1] is pleased to leave me waiting,
Or decrees that I ride or run on his errand,

1. An earthly feudal lord.

What does grumbling gain me but greater anger?
If, despite my desire, he gives slight care to me,
And I put up with pain and displeasure as reward,
I have bowed at his bidding and brought myself profit.

Did not Jonah in Judah once so juggle with his fate?
To be certain of success, he stupidly erred.
Tarry a little time, attend to me awhile:
I shall utter it all as the Holy Book tells.

I

It occurred in the confines of the country of Judah
That Jonah was enjoined to be prophet to the Gentiles:
The great word of God, no gladness bringing,
Sounded to him sternly, saying in his ear:

'Bestir yourself, and set out forthwith,
With not another word, for the Nineveh highway,
And sow in that city my sayings everywhere,
Which, proper to the place, I shall put in your heart.

'I am well aware of the wickedness of its people,
And their devilry is so deep I shall indulge it no more,
But take revenge for their villainy and vileness at once.
Now go there at great speed and give them my message!'

When the sounding voice stopped, which had stunned his mind,
The brain of Jonah burned, and rebelliously he thought,
'If I bow to his bidding and bring them such words,
And they seize me, my sorrows shall start in Nineveh!

'He tells me those traitors are extremely wicked:
If I tell them these tidings, they will take me at once,
Pen me in prison, put me in the stocks,
Twist me in tortures, and tweak out my eyes.

'A marvellous message for a man to preach
Among so many and such murderous enemies!
If my gracious God would give me such grief,
Deeming my death to be due for some crime,

'In spite of all peril, I shall approach it no nearer,
But hurry somewhere else, out of his sight.
I shall turn my steps to Tarshish, and stay there a while,
And so lost, I shall be left alone by him, perhaps.'

Jonah then jumped up and went to Joppa,
Petulantly complaining, as he approached the port,
That nothing could inure him to those noxious pains,
Though the Father who formed him made free with his fate.

'So high', said he, 'our heavenly King sits
In his glittering glory that his glance takes in little,
Though I be snared in Nineveh and stripped naked,
Or roughly be rent on the cross by a rout of ruffians.'

So, passing to the port, he looked for a passage,
Found there a fair ship fit for its voyage,
Made contract with the crew and counted out the payment
For taking him to Tarshish at topmost speed.

Then they trimmed their tackle as he took his place on deck,
Caught up the cross-sail, coiled in the cables,
Quickly with the windlass weighed their anchors,
Bound to the bowsprit the bowline from the mast,

Gathered in the guide-ropes as the great mainsail fell,
Lugged it to larboard, laid the ship downwind,
And the blithe breath at their back bosomed out the cross-sail
And wafted this sweet ship swiftly from the haven.

Then was Jonah the most joyful Jew that ever was,
To have passed so promptly from the peril of God;
Holding that he who created all earth
Was powerless to pain a passenger on the sea!

Ah, foolish fellow to refuse to suffer,
Now put in peril of a plight much worse!
A hapless hope had he that God,
Who sought him in Samaria, could see no farther;

But fitly God looked forth far and wide.
Yet often had Jonah heard the holy saying
Of deathless King David, on dais enthroned,
Who said in a psalm which he set in the Psalter:

'You fools among the folk, face this fact
And understand it early: high he may be,
But does he who made all ears not hear, you think?
It cannot be that he is blind who built all eyes.'

But, drooping in dotage, the man dreaded no blow,
Far faring afloat on the flood-tide to Tarshish;
And truly in no time at all he was overtaken,
Shamefully falling short when he shot at his target:

For the Wielder of Wisdom, wise in all things,
Ever wakeful and waiting, works things at will.
He called on the craft he had carved with his hands,
And the winds stirred the more savagely when sternly he called:

'Eurus and Aquilon[1] in the east abiding,
Blow both at my bidding on the blear waters!'
There was no time between his telling and their doing,
So prompt were the pair to prosecute his command.

The tumult of tempest started in the north-east
As both the winds blew on the blear waters.
Racks of storm rose over roaring thunder,
The stricken sea soughed, most strange to hear,

And gales on the grim water, together conflicting,
Sent the wild waves whelming high,
Then battering to the abyss, where the bedded fishes,
For the raging roughness round them, dared rest nowhere.

Where wind and water and weak ship met,
No joke did Jonah judge it then,
For the vessel reeled around on the rough waves.
A sea from behind struck them, smashing the gear,

And hurling in a heap the helm and the stern.
Ropes snapped asunder, so did the mast,
The sail swayed into the sea, the small boat
Quaffed the cold water, and a cry went up.

Yet they cut the cords and cast out the cargo;
Boldly and busily they baled and threw out,
Scooping the evil sea as it strove to escape them,
For lamentable though his load be, man's life is sweet.

Bales went overboard as they busily threw out
Their baggage, feather beds and brilliant robes,
Their charged coffers, their chests, and their chains as well.
Should calm ever come, their craft would be lighter.

---

1. Eurus is the east wind, Aquilon the north wind.

But still ever stronger rose the sounds of the gale,
And the waters ever wilder, the waves more furious.
Sunk in exhaustion, the sailors lost all hope,
But each groaned to the god he could gain from best.

Some to Vernagu[1] avouched their vows solemnly,
To the holy maid Diana, or to hardy Neptune,
To Mahound or to Magog, the Moon and the Sun,
And each lad where he loved and had laid his heart.

Then the sprightliest spoke up, despair in his heart;
'I believe some liar here, some lawless wretch,
Has grieved his god and got here among us.
We all sink for his sin, for his sake perish!

'I believe we should lay lots on every man,
And then heave him overboard who has the loss;
Then the guilt being gone, we must grant it likely
That the god of this great storm will give the rest pity.'

They sealed their assent and assembled forthwith,
Clambering from corners to catch their destinies.
Down the hatches an ocean pilot hurriedly leapt
To seek out more sailors and send them to the lottery.

He failed with no fellow that he found below
But for Jonah the Jew who secretly slept.
He had fled for fear of the frenzied sea
To the bilge of the boat: on a board he lay,

Huddled by the hurrock[2] from the anger of heaven
In sluggish sleep, slobbering and snoring.
The man ordered him up with a hearty kick:
'May Raguel the fettered fiend rouse you from dreams!'

Seizing hold of his hair, he haled him out,
Dragged him on deck, dumped him down
And in rage arraigned him: what reason had he
To sleep so soundly in such a crisis?

---

1. 'Vernagu is an enormous black giant who comes forward to challenge the paladins of Charlemagne' (Bateson). Magog is the name of the Scythian race of Giants, mentioned in Ezekiel XXXVIII, of whom Gog was chief prince. Mahound is of course Mahomet, whose crescent moon is the emblem on the Moslem flag: the poet is concerned to place Jonah among unbelievers. Unlike Diana and Neptune, none of these three persons is divine.
2. An Orkney word, apparently meaning the after part of the keel.

Swiftly they settled their several lots,
And the least of the lots was selected by Jonah.
With clamorous question, they quickly asked him,
'What the devil have you done, you doltish lout?

'What do you seek by sea, you sinful evil-doer,
To lose us all our lives by your loathsome crimes?
Have you no governor, no god to give your prayers to,
That you sluggishly slumber at your slaying-time?

'What country, what cause do you claim as yours?
Wherever it is, what errand are you on?
We deem you a dead man for your devilish deeds,
So give glory to your god, and get you hence!'

'I am a Hebrew,' said he, 'in Israel born.
The high god I honour made everything there is,
All the world and the welkin, the winds and the stars,
And all dwellers therein, with one great word.

'Destruction is raging now by reason of me,
For I have grieved my god and my guilt is clear.
So carry me to the scuppers and cast me overboard,
Or your fortunes will fail, I firmly believe.'

He made signs to the sailors, who sensed his meaning,
That he had fled from before the face of the Lord.
Then fear fell on them, frightening their souls,
And they raced to have him rowing, ranging off alone.

Seamen went speedily for stout long oars
For rowing, since the rigging had been wrenched overboard.
They heaved and hauled to help them up,
But the device was in vain and availed them nothing.

The seething of the storm-seas snapped the oars,
And their hands were empty of helping means.
No comfort was to be come by, no counsel at all
But that judgement come to Jonah, justice forthwith.

First they prayed to the Prince whom prophets serve
To grant them his grace, that they should give him no offence,
Thus in blameless blood bathing their hands,
Though he were his whom here they were to kill.

By top and by toe they took him at once then,
And promptly pitched him into the appalling depths:
And he being hurled out, the hurricane ended,
And quickly calm came to the waters.

Though the rigging was rent and dragging overboard,
Quick-running currents kept them for a time
Ever drifting off in the open sea,
Till a sweet wind wafted them swiftly towards land.

As they came to the coast, they choired their praise
In the manner of Moses to our merciful God,
Setting up sacrifices, solemnly vowing,
And granting true godhead to God alone.

Joyful their jubilation: but Jonah, terrified,
Though set against suffering, was still in jeopardy,
For the fate of the fellow when flung into the sea
Would stupefy the senses, were it not stated in the Bible.

II

Now is Jonah the Jew judged to be drowned,
For sharply men had shoved him from the ship in distress.
But a wild rolling whale, by warrant of Fate
Beaten up from the abyss, by the boat was floating,

And sensing that sea-goer in search of the depths,
Swiftly glided with gaping gorge to gobble him up.
His feet they still held fast when the fish so seized him,
And without touching a tooth, he tumbled down its throat.

The sea-monster swung away and swept to the bottom
By the sifting surge-floor where stark rocks reared,
With the man in his maw, amazed in dread –
Little wonder it was that woe tortured him!

For had not the mighty hand of high heaven's King
Guarded this guilty one in the guts of hell,
What belief could one allow, by any law of nature,
In a lease of life so long inside there?

By the Lord on throne aloft his life was saved,
Though forlorn of fortune in the fish's belly,
And driven through the deep, darkly wallowing.
Lord, cold was his comfort and cruel his care!

For each part of his plight was plainly apparent –
From craft to quivering sea, then caught by a monster
And thrown down its throat as a thing no more compressed
Than mote entering minster door, so mighty its gullet!

He glided in near the gills, through greasy slime,
Whirled along the weasand as wide as a road,
Ever head over heels hurrying along the gut
Till he staggered into a space like an extensive hall.

There he found his feet and fumbled about,
Standing up in the stomach, which stank like the devil.
In the grease and the grime there, as ghastly as hell,
His sojourn was set, safe from harm.

Furtively he felt about to find the best place
In every nook by the navel, but nowhere found
Any rest or remedy: reeking ooze
Gurgled in every gut: yet God is sweet.

There to calmness he came at last, and called to the Lord,
'Now Prince, take pity upon your prophet!
Though I am foolish and fickle, and false in my heart,
Make void your vengeance by virtue of your mercy!

'Though I sinned in deceit, the scum of all prophets,
You are God, and garner all good to yourself:
Have mercy on your man and his misdemeanours,
And assert yourself Sovereign of sea and land!'

With that he climbed to a corner and kept still there,
Where no filth or defilement could flow about him,
And sat as safe and sound, except for the gloom,
As in the bowels of the boat, where he had been asleep before.

So in the belly of the beast he breathed in safety
Three days and three nights, ever thinking of the Lord,
His might and his mercy, and his moderation also.
He, estranged from God when safe, in his suffering now knew him.

In the welter of the deep wastes the whale ever rolled
Through raging ocean regions, rank in his will,
For that mote in his maw, small though it was,
Made his heart heave, for all his hugeness.

Sailing on the surge in safety, Jonah heard
The mighty billows beating on the beast's back and sides,
And the prophet proffered a prayer forthwith,
Phrased as follows: profuse were his words:

'Lord, in my calamity I lifted my voice
From hell's womb-hole here, and you heard my utterance.
I called, and you caught my obscure cry,
Conducting me from the depths to the dark heart.

'The fierce flow of your flood folded me round;
The flux of your foaming gulfs and fathomless deeps
And the clashing currents from countless channels
In one weltering wave washed me about.

'Yet still I can say, sitting near the sea-bed,
"In my affliction I am flung from before your bright eyes,
Sundered from sight of you; but certain is my hope
Of treading your temple again, attaching my faith to you."

'I am steeped in the surge till my sufferings stupefy me;
My body is bound by the abyss about me;
The swirling of pure water whirls about my head;
Past the limits of the last mountain I lie fallen.

'The ramparts of every ridge rigorously restrain me,
So that land is lost to reach, and my life is in your hands.
You shall succour your servant, while sleep lulls your justice,
Through the might of your mercy, which is much to be trusted.

'For when the access of anguish was hidden in my soul,
The justice of my generous Lord jumped to my mind,
And I prayed that in pity for his prophet he would hear,
And that my orison might enter his holy house.

'I have communed with your mighty works many a long day,
But I am firm in my faith now that foolhardy people
Who vow their lives to vanities and to vain things
Amounting to mere nothing, find mercy is away.

'But devoutly I vow, and in very truth affirm it,
Solemnly to sacrifice to you when my safety is assured,
And to offer you a holy gift for my happy fortune,
And to carry out your behests: here is my promise!'

Then fiercely our Father ordered the fish
Promptly to spew him out upon dry land.
The whale turned at God's will towards the coast
And ejected Jonah there, as enjoined by the Lord.

He strode out of the sea in his soiled clothes –
Well might he demand that his mantle be washed!
The land that he looked at, lying before him,
Was precisely the same that he had forsworn earlier.

III

The gust of God's word then again upbraided him:
'Will you never go to Nineveh, not for anything?'
'I shall go, Lord. Give me your grace,' said Jonah.
'My only gain is to go, so giving you pleasure.'

'Rise, approach then to preach: the place is here.
Lo, my word is locked in you! Let it loose there!'
Then up he rose and went off at urgent speed,
And came near that same night to Nineveh itself,

A city so spacious and astoundingly wide
That to thread one's way through it was a three days' task.
In just one day's journey, Jonah never stopped,
Not speaking to a soul a single word.

Then he clamorously cried out, making clear to all
The true tenor of his tidings, telling them this:
'Yet forty days in full shall fare to their ending,
Then shall Nineveh be nothing, an annihilated city.

'This town most truly shall totter to the ground:
Upside down you shall be driven to the deep abyss,
To be swallowed up swiftly by the swarthy earth,
And all who live here shall lose their life's sweetness!'

This speech was reported and spread abroad
To burghers and bold knights abiding in the town.
Such terror then took them, such torturing dread,
Their cheeks' colour changed with the chill at their hearts.

But still Jonah ceased not, ever saying the same:
'God's anger shall utterly empty this place!'
Then the people most piteously prayed in quiet,
And with great dread of God grieved in their hearts.

They got hold of rough hairshirts which harshly bit into them,[1]
Binding them to their backs and their bare flanks,
Dropped dust on their heads and in desolation begged
That he be pleased by their penance, their repentance for sins.

Jonah clamoured in that country till the king heard.
He rapidly rose and ran from his throne,
Ripping off his rich robe, rendering his back naked,
And hurried right into a heap of ashes.

He called harshly for a hairshirt and hastily donned it,
Sewed on it some sackcloth, and sighed wretchedly.
There he lay dazed in the dust, dropping his tears,
Most wonderfully bewailing his wicked deeds.

Then 'Assemble speedily!' he said to his officers.
'Put out this edict, which I issue myself:
All living things lying in the limits of the city,
Both men and beasts, women, babes and children,

'Every prince, every priest, and prelates as well,
Must fast in full measure for their offending sins.
Sever infants from their suckling, sad though it make them.
Beasts shall not browse on broom or herbs,

'Nor go to their grazing on grassy pasture:
No ox shall have hay, or horse have water.
Famished for lack of food, we shall furiously pray,
And the sound shall ascend to the Dispenser of Pity.

'What happens or may happen but by order of God,
Great in his goodness and forgiving grace?
In spite of his displeasure, so plentiful is his power
That he may find mercy in his mild gentleness.

'And if we cease to sport in our sins so abhorrent,
And peacefully pace the path appointed by God,
He will abate his burning fury and blunt his wrath,
And forgive us our guilt – if we grant him to be God.'

---

1. 'And next his flesh he wore hard hair, full of knots, which was his shirt.
And his breech was of the same, and the knots sticked fast within the skin,
and all his body full of worms; he suffered great pain' (description of Thomas
à Becket, from Caxton's translation of 'The Golden Legend', written by
Jacobus de Voragine, Archbishop of Genoa, in about 1275).

All obeyed his bidding, abandoned their sins,
And completed their penance at the prince's command;
And God in his goodness forgave, as the king said:
Though his oath bound him otherwise, he withheld vengeance.

IV

Much misery this made for the man Jonah;
He raged like roaring gale with wrath against God:
Such anger struck hot to his heart that he cried
In his pain a prayer to the high Prince, in these words:

'I beseech you, Sire, be yourself the judge!
Has not what I uttered happened now,
What I cried in my own country, when you decreed that I
Should travel to this town and tell your purpose?

'Well was I aware of your wise sufferance,
Your gentleness, your justice, your generous grace,
Your tolerance of turpitude, your tardy vengeance.
For however foul the offence, sufficient is your mercy.

'I did not doubt, when I had done my best
To menace the proud men of this mighty city,
That with prayer and penance they could purchase peace:
Hence my fury to flee far into Tarshish.

'Now Lord, take my life, for it lasts too long;
Be prompt with my last pangs, put me to death,
For it seems to me sweeter to cease life at once
Than to keep proclaiming your decrees and coming to grief.'

The speech of our Sovereign then sounded in his ear,
In burning rebuke upbraiding the prophet:
'Mark me, man! Is your mad mood just
For any deed I have done, or doom I have decreed you?'

So, joylessly jarring, Jonah arose,
Set off for the eastern edge of the high capital,
And being concerned to see how the city would fare,
He prepared on the plain a point of vantage.

There he built himself a booth, the best that he could,
Of hay and evergreen and a handful of herbs;
For that waste was wanting in waving groves
Which could guard from the glare or give any shade.

He bent under his little booth, his back to the sun,
And in sadness there slumbered and slept all night,
While God through his grace made to grow from the ground
A most comely creeper, which coiled above him.

At dawn of the day which the dread Lord sent,
The sleeper stirred beneath the soaring gourd,
Then gazed at the greenness of the glimmering leaves:
Such a bower of bliss no human ever had.

For it was broad at the base, and above, domed,
Walled in on either side, as a house might be,
With a narrow opening to the north, and nowhere else,
All close like a coppice which coolly shades.

Jonah gazed on the green and graceful leaves,
Waving all the while in the wind cool and mild.
The sheer sunlight shone on it, but no shaft could,
To the extent of a tiny mote, touch the man within.

Then happy was he with his haven so beautiful,
Lying inside lounging, looking at the city,
So content with his trusty gourd, tumbling about beneath it,
That devil a bit for his diet that day cared he.

As he looked at his lodgement, he laughed all the time,
And had a wish for such a home in his own country,
On high on Mount Ephraim or the hills of Hermon:
'A worthier dwelling I never wished to possess!'

And when night-time neared and he needed to sleep,
Soundly into slumber he slipped beneath the leaves.
But God raised a reptile to ravage its roots,
So that when the man awoke, the woodbine was withered.

Next he warned the west to awaken most softly,
And instructed Zephyrus[1] to scorch with his breath,
That no cloud might quicken to occlude the sunrise,
With its beams as brilliant as a burning candle.

Then awaking from the whims of his wilful dreams,
Jonah gazed at the gourd, now gone in destruction;
All cankered and decayed the comely leaves,
Scorched by the sun before the sleeper was aware.

1. Zephyrus is the west wind.

The torrid heat stirred, most terribly burning,
The warm wind from the west withered the herbs,
And the grieving man on the ground could get no shade:
His gourd was gone, and groaning, he wept.

Then raging with wrath, he roared hotly,
'Ah, Maker of Man, what mastery is this,
To single out your servant for special destruction?
Why me for all the mischief your might can make?

'I salved myself with a solace now snatched from me,
My gourd so graceful which guarded my head;
But now I see that you are set to steal my comfort:
Why not doom me to death? My life endures too long.'

In reply to the prophet then spoke the Lord:
'Is it right, you rash man, to raise such a din,
To fly so fast into fury for a creeper?
Why so peevish, prophet, for so paltry a thing?'

'Hardly paltry,' Jonah replied, 'but proper to this:
I wish I were away from the world, in the grave.'
'If it grieves you,' said God, 'then give this a thought:
If I help on my handiwork, have no wonder.

'You have become most choleric on account of a creeper,
But you attended to it for no time at all.
It flourished in one flash and faded in the next.
Yet it fascinates you so foully, you would forfeit your life.

'Then blame me not for business whose benefit I desire,
But allow grace to the misguided who regret their sins.
I created them all of primordial matter,
Watched over them afterwards and helped them a long time.

'Should I lose the labour of·this lengthy task,
And destroy that city when its sins were repented,
The pains of so precious a place would penetrate my heart,
So many wicked men are now mourning in it.

'And among these many are some mad, yet innocent,
Such as babes at the breast, blameless of evil,
And witless women, not wise enough to tell
One hand from the other, for all this high world;

Or to realize that the rung and the riser are different;
That a rule recognizes the right hand of man
And his left: though a life be lost for not knowing.

'Besides, the city swarms with dumb beasts
Not able to err and lose heart on account of it.
What reason have I to rage at true penitents
Who come to acclaim me king, my counsel their faith?

'Were I as hasty as you here, harm would follow:
Were my sufferance so scanty, scarcely could men thrive.
I might not be called merciful, manifesting such malice,
For mastery cannot be managed unless mercy temper it.

'Be less furious, my fine fellow, and fare you forth!
Be brave and forbearing in bitterness and joy,
For he who rashly rages and rips his clothes
Must then sit with the torn stuff and sew it together.'

So when Poverty oppresses me with pains in plenty,
It shall become me in quiet and calm to suffer;
In pain and in penance to prove plainly
That Patience is a princely thing, though displeasing often.

Pearl

'Pearl' appears first of the four related poems on the unique manu-
script Cotton Nero A.x. The language is of the north-west, possibly
of the border area between Cheshire and Northern Staffordshire, and
internal evidence in the four poems, concerning costume, castle
architecture, and so forth, taken together with the style of the hand-
writing, places the composition late in the fourteenth century. The
two virtues of which 'Pearl' treats, Purity and Forbearance, each
receive fuller treatment by the poet, in 'Cleanness' and 'Patience'
respectively, so that 'Pearl' might appear to be the forerunner of
those poems. However, its poetic mastery, and its mingling of
French prosodical elements with the traditional English ones, seem
to place it after them. Moreover, its loftier treatment of the two
virtues makes 'Pearl' appear in fact as a consolidation of the ideas in
'Cleanness' and 'Patience'. 'Pearl' is a greater achievement than the
same poet's romance, *Sir Gawain and the Green Knight*, and just as
Sir Gawain must be considered one of the best narrative poems in
English, so his 'Pearl' ranks among our finest elegies. Indeed, I can
see no grounds for preferring 'Lycidas' or 'Adonais', and offer my
inadequate translation of 'Pearl' as the most important work in this
book.

Although several different approaches to the task of translation
were made, and the poem was worked in its entirety in two different
modes, it proved impossible to be utterly faithful to the complex
form of the original. A description of the form the poet chose may
show why this was so. Each of his hundred and one twelve-line
stanzas has the rhyme scheme ababababbcbc, and most lines contain
alliteration of at least two stressed syllables: in addition, each group
of five stanzas is bound by a link-word which ends one stanza and is
the first stress-word in the next. The groups of stanzas thus linked
are usually units of sense: one group contains six stanzas, and so
enables the poet to make his stanza total a hundred and one, a number
to which he seemed to attach some importance, for *Sir Gawain* has
the same number. (For discussion of this, see Appendix Two of *Sir*

Gawain and the Green Knight in the Penguin Classics translation, pages 128–9.) The line itself is often iambic, but may contain from seven to thirteen syllables: it is a compromise between the four-beat alliterative line of Old English and the regular iambic of Romance prosody.

In the translation, a more modest rhyme scheme of ababcdcddede has been adopted, force perforce, as a basis, but where possible it has been improved on, and in seven stanzas the original rhyme scheme has been maintained; but all the other characteristics of the original versification remain, and probably its alliterative content has been exceeded.

The extraordinary formal beauty of the stanza extends to the whole poem, which achieves strict harmony between passionate grief, lofty moral vision, and mystical experience. These are the heart of the poem, and at the end they resolve their counterpoint, which proceeds always with gravity and grace, in a finale of consolation, hope and benediction.

The poem opens with the poet sorrowing beside the grave of his lost Pearl, content only in his grief (stanzas 1–4). There he swoons (5), and in his dream, finds himself in a marvellous countryside, on the bank of a stream (6–10) which, he surmises, separates him from the castle of Paradise. Beyond the stream he sees a beautiful girl (11–15), clad in white and adorned with pearls. She is the Pearl whom he has lost. She approaches him (16–20), and the poet expresses his grief. She rebukes him for sorrowing, seeing that she is now immortal. The poet rejoices at his reunion with her (21–25). Pearl explains that only his death can reunite them, and opposes his renewed lamentation with advice that he should submit to God's will (26–30). The poet apologizes, and she explains that now she is a queen in heaven (31–35). The poet doubts that one who died so young could rival Our Lady, the only Queen (36–41), but Pearl, citing the parable of the Vineyard, proves her right to immortal life (42–49). He objects that she has not earned it; she explains not only that the grace of God encompasses, besides the innocent, the reformed sinner who strives towards heaven, but that Jesus insisted on a child-like quality in those who enter the Kingdom (50–62). The poet cannot understand why she alone is the bride of Christ, and she answers that she is but one of the many brides described in the Apocalypse (63–66). She proceeds to extol the meekness (67),

Passion (67–8), Baptism (69), and present triumphal state (69–70) of Christ, and describes the life of bliss in the New Jerusalem (71–75). The poet humbly asks how Pearl is so far from Jerusalem (76–78), to which she replies that the City of God is not the same as the old Jerusalem (79–80). The poet asks her to take him to the New Jerusalem, but she says that only the pure may set foot in it (81). However, she guides him to where he may see it (82). Enraptured at the sight, he describes it in detail (83–91), and then becomes aware of a procession of heavenly maidens, led by the Lamb (92–3). The Elders do honour to the Lamb, and while the song of heaven is sung (94), the poet contemplates the bleeding wounds of Christ (95): yet these do not mar Christ's joy and glory (96). The poet sees his own Pearl among the maidens (96) and, frenzied with longing, resolves to go to her, though the attempt bring death (97). God breaks the vision, and the poet awakes in awe (98–9). He resolves to behave as Pearl had advised, and in calm of mind submitting to the will of God, prays that he in turn may deserve the blessed life.

The dream-vision was a standard device of medieval writers, and therefore needs no introduction to readers familiar with the mechanism of, say, *La Divina Commedia* or *Piers Plowman*. Macrobius, who commented on Cicero's *Somnium Scipionis* in the fifth century, seems to have started the vogue, and his name is mentioned at the start of *Le Roman de la Rose*. Besides being a means of launching a story, the dream was often a medium for the utterance of serious and especially religious matters, for the power of which the apparently supernatural quality of dream was warranty. Dream was out of consciousness and therefore an extension of the mind beyond life; an extension which, in all periods before the modern, might lead to truth or falsehood: Greek legend had the Gates of Dreams, an ivory one and a horn one, from which, respectively, false and true dreams emerged. So the dream could be invaded by devils or other betrayers; but when it was possessed by God or any of his emissaries in beatific vision, the awoken dreamer would prize the memory beyond conscious experience or meditation. At a more popular level, the dream could readily present marvel, the basis of most medieval fiction.

The main marvels in the poem are the paradisal land in which the poet finds himself after swooning, and the vision within a vision, of the New Jerusalem, which he sees before returning to consciousness. Their two sources, the literature of Romance and the Bible, are drawn on continuously, with the result that a work in the courtly tradition, with all that that implies of subtleties of dealing between persons and intensities of personal emotion, emerges as a mystical didactic poem of general application. In the hundred years since the appearance of the first printed edition of 'Pearl', the debate concerning whether the main intention of the poet was to express personal grief or to write a religious allegory has tended to obscure the double impact of the work. One cannot complete a reading of the poem – indeed, one can hardly start it – without knowing the poignancy of the writer's personal sorrow; and it is his experience of grief that gives intensity to his rapture at the vision of the New Jerusalem, and validity to his didactic conclusion.

In this profound work, in which the two conventions strike echoes and depths from each other, the Virgin Mary figures as 'the Queen of Courtesy' (stanza 37). Now this title properly belongs to the chief lady of a Romance court, like the shadowy Guinevere, or the real Eleanor of Aquitaine, who was in the twelfth century 'the richest heiress of Western Christendom', and 'the presiding genius ... of courtly culture' (Friedrich Heer, *The Medieval World*, page 123). But the 'Pearl' poet is not confusing the quality of the Queen of Heaven with that of earthly beings. He is thinking of the spirit of divine grace, as Saint Paul defines it in his First Epistle to the Corinthians (chapter XII), the celestial exemplar of the highest earthly grace to which human society can attain. Then the manner of conduct and address used between Pearl and the poet are according to strict courtly canon. She greets him 'inclining low as a maiden may', and calls him 'Sir', just as a well-brought-up child should. Yet Pearl's utterance is limited to doctrine, for she is a glorified soul who must express the eternal truths relative to the situation of her suppliant. Accordingly, there is no daughterly unbending, or sympathy with the poet, even in his most dejected moments. The radiant but de-personalized emissary of God and the grief-stricken poet-parent convince in their different ways, and complement each other.

The doctrinal message which Pearl conveys to him is orthodox except in one or two small details, and it will not be enlarged on here. Those interested are referred to pages xix-xxvii of the Oxford edition of 'Pearl' (Professor E. V. Gordon) and the select bibliography on page liii. There also, on pages 165-7, will be found a list of the ninety-nine biblical quotations or allusions in the poem. It may be worth emphasizing that the penny which is the reward of the labourers in the vineyard represents eternal life itself, so that no rewarding by God according to varying deserts would make theological sense: whatever one's experience or accomplishments, one is saved by grace, or not saved. In his picture of the hereafter, the poet differs from Dante, who follows Aquinas and medieval orthodoxy generally in assigning, in his *Paradiso*, different degrees of blessed perfection, degrees which paradoxically do not affect the supreme bliss of each soul. Presumably a feudal age had to continue earthly hierarchies in its heaven: our poet is content to follow the letter of Christ's teaching. His point also illuminates the answer to another doubt raised by the Dreamer: how a child of barely two could achieve such exaltation immediately she entered heaven. The tradition, strong in the Middle Ages, was that any infant dying before committing a sin might be ranked with the Holy Innocents, the children slaughtered by Herod. 'That they could with orthodoxy be included in the company of the Lamb', states Professor Gordon, 'is shown by the use of Apocalypse xiv, 1–5 as the lesson for the mass of the Holy Innocents, 28 December.' The short step from general innocence (of infants) to special purity (of virgins) is easily made, and Pearl herself enfolds the two types in a single statement in stanza 71:

> So every soul unsullied by wrong
> Makes for the Lamb a worthy wife.

Yet Pearl's purpose in so enlightening her questioner is to convince him of her status, and hence of her right to teach him his main lesson: that he must learn humbly to suffer the will of God. But the questioner's first purpose is not to seek doctrinal enlightenment; it is to discover the fate of his beloved in the after-life. His satisfaction that she is

> To the circle of all the blessed assigned

is the tranquil centre of his final resolve to please his Prince's mind by being a true servant.

And so to the gem which dominates and unifies the poem with its multiple symbolism, and thus provides a natural title: the Pearl itself. Other precious substances, stone or mineral, were hacked from earth or rock, and with their hardness, glint, or weight, chiefly moved men's minds to thoughts of wealth, magical power, ostentation; but pearl, mysterious offering of the sea, unique in substance, seems to have aroused from the first, besides the conventional associations and practices of value, visionary man's predilection for symbol. And although other gems have had various symbolical associations in different cultures, the pearl, perhaps because of its whiteness, is almost constant in its representation of preciousness, purity, modesty, spiritual perfection. Indeed, its virtues seem curiously attuned to the spirituality of the Christian message, so that it became, in the Middle Ages, the characteristically Christian gem (contrast the ancient Hindu exaltation of the ruby, a red stone which became the Lord of Gems because it contained an inextinguishable flame and preserved the bodily and mental health of the wearer). Medieval lapidaries in general are based on the scriptural mention of jewels,[1] and the symbolism of the pearl derives ultimately from 'the pearl of great price', which the merchant in the parable bought, selling all he possessed in order to obtain it. The pearl of the parable is the glorious perfection of heavenly life; the Dreamer sees it on Pearl's breast (stanza 19), and the beatified girl identifies it in the peroration of her sermon on the parable of the vineyard (stanzas 61–2).

As the symbol of spiritual purity, the pearl became also the symbol of virginity, and of pure womanhood generally: 'Margarita' (the word means 'pearl') is found as early as the third century as a woman's name, and the Middle Ages produced several Margarets, all successors of the third-century saint of Antioch. To the mystical sense of physical purity which came into Christianity in Pauline and

1. The ideas of Rabanus Maurus, Archbishop of Mainz (786–856), quoted by George F. Kunz in *The Curious Lore of Precious Stones*, express medieval developments of thought: 'In the jasper is figured the truth of faith; in the sapphire the height of celestial hope; in the chalcedony, the flame of inner charity. In the emerald is expressed the strength of faith in adversity; in the sardonyx, the humility of the saints in spite of their virtues; in the sard, the venerable blood of the martyrs. In the chrysolite, indeed, is shown true spiritual preaching accompanied by miracles; in the beryl, the perfect operation of prophecy; in the topaz, the ardent contemplation of the prophecies. Lastly, in the chrysoprase is demonstrated the work of the blessed martyrs and their reward; in the hyacinth, the celestial rapture of the learned in their high thoughts and their humble descent to human things out of regard for the weak; in the amethyst, the constant thought of the heavenly kingdom in humble souls.' Saint Hildegarde, who died in 1179, also has much to say about the Christian values of precious stones.

later times, non-Christian gnosticism contributed, as it did to the religious symbolism of the pearl, and it is probably from such sources that the idea of the pearl as the purified soul came.

At first in the poem, the pearl is given the conventional praise due to a precious object which will delight a prince: the 'fine', the 'radiant', the 'without a spot' are only later to be charged with spiritual meaning. Now the magical notion of the gem develops, with the description of the beneficent herbs and flowers which spring from the place 'where Pearl drove down to the dark of earth'; and now too, Pearl becomes a person, a lost loved one to be mourned. The marvellous region in which the Dreamer soon finds himself differs from the courtly lovers' Garden of Delight in one essential respect – the radiance of holy jewels makes it a spiritual place, where the very gravel he treads is pearl. Against this unearthly background appears Pearl herself, a living symbol of the purity of female saints. The pearl becomes the immaculate soul, into which Pearl changed when she ceased to be 'a mere rose', or mortal girl. The crown of pearl which she wears is explained as a symbol of her virginity, and her pearl-trimmed dress represents her freedom from all taint.

In the vision of the New Jerusalem, pearl has pride of place over all other jewels. The twelve layers of the foundations are each of a separate precious stone, and the shining walls are of jasper; but the gates, the twelve ever-open gates, through which souls triumphant in virtue may enter, are made of 'that pearl whose purity never abates'. And the spotless pearl is the crest of all the consorts of the Lamb in the celestial city: the whiteness of their attire is also the whiteness and perfection of the body of Christ, out of which and over which flows the blood of redemption and glory – a contrast and a shock, perfect in doctrine and art, to the pearl-inspired whiteness of the rest of the poem.

A second sight of his own Pearl, whom 'love-longing's great delight' tempts him to describe this time as his 'little queen' although he knows her now to be God's, drives the Dreamer to attempt to join her without first winning God's grace. But when the dream is broken, the pearl asserts its symbolism, and the poet, echoing the first line of his poem, resolves to be, not a jewel to please an earthly prince, but a pearl, that is, a purified soul, to please the Prince of Heaven.

71

PEARL

1

1   Pearl, delighting a prince's pleasure,
    Chastely imprisoned in purest gold!
    There never came a costlier treasure
    From all the East, I firmly hold;
    So fine, so smooth on every side,
    So round, so radiant, however set,
    That I gave this Pearl the place of pride
    Above all jewels I judged as yet.
        Alas! In a garden I lost it, let
        It go to the ground on a grassy plot.
        Bereft of love, I am racked by regret
        For Pearl, my own Pearl without a spot.

2   Since in that spot from me it sprung,
    I have waited there often, in want of that wealth
    That once was wont to rout all wrong
    And heave on high my luck and health.
    That weighs on my heart with woes profound
    And burns my heart with baneful power;
    Yet never in song came sweeter sound
    Than stole on me in that silent hour:
        For thoughts came thronging to the garden bower
        Of its beauty, clogged in clayey clot.
        O earth, a jewel of joy you mar –
        Pearl, my own Pearl without a spot.

3   That spot of fragrant herbs must spread,
    Seeing such riches there rot and decay.
    Blossoms white and blue and red
    Must shine and shimmer in the sun's ray;
    To flower and fruit no blight shall cling
    Where Pearl drove down to the dark of earth;
    For grain so dying, the grasses spring,
    Else how could wheat have harvest worth?
        All good begins from good at birth:
        So fair a seed must fail not,
        But send out spices springing forth
        From that precious Pearl without a spot.

4   To the spot I speak of with sad reason
    I entered in that garden green,
    In festive August, the high season,
    When corn is cut with sickles keen.
    The grave where Pearl had gone from view
    Was shadowed with herbs of lovely sheen,
    Ginger, gillyflower, gromwell[1] too,
    And spreading peonies[2] scattered between.
      If that sight was fair to be seen,
      Yet fairer the fragrance from the plot.
      There dwells, I swear, that one serene,
      My precious Pearl without a spot.

5   Beside that spot my hands I clenched,
    Cold with gripping care and grief;
    Deafening dolour my spirit drenched,
    Though reason proffered right relief.
    In fierce conflicting questioning,
    And pain that Pearl should prisoner dwell,
    My soul yet sank in suffering,
    Though counsels of Christ all care dispel.
      There on that flowery patch I fell:
      Such fragrant balm to my brain then shot,
      I slipped into a swooning spell
      For that precious Pearl without a spot.

II

6   From that spot my spirit sprang into space:
    My body remained on the mound in trance.
    My soul had gone, by God's own grace,
    Adventuring where all marvels chance.
    I knew not where in the world was the place,
    But, cast among cliffs that clove to a height,
    Towards a forest I set my face,
    Where rich-hued crags came into sight.
      No mortal would believe their light,
      A gleaming glory glinting out:
      No webs men weave were ever so bright,
      So dazzlingly adorned about.

1. Its seed was considered to be pearl-shaped.
2. A herb of the Sun, potent against melancholy. The conclusion of the poem demonstrates the perfection of this artifice, which makes peonies grow all over the grave of Pearl.

7   Adorned were all the hillsides there
    With crystal cliffs, while down below
    Brilliant woodlands were everywhere.
    The boles were as blue as indigo;
    Like burnished silver the leaves swayed,
    Quivering close on the branches spread;
    They shimmered in splendour, glanced and played,
    When glinting gleams from the sky were shed.
        The gravel I ground beneath my tread
        Of precious orient pearl was formed:
        A sunbeam's light would be dull and dead
        When set by a scene so brightly adorned.

8   The adornment of those uplands fair
    Made my spirit forget to grieve.
    Such freshly flavoured fruits were there
    That the food fairly made me revive.
    Birds in flocks, of flaming hues,
    Both large and small, flew in the glade;
    Melody matching their radiant muse
    No singing citherner ever played,
        So sweet the harmony their song conveyed
        As they warbled wonderfully, winging the air.
        Such marvellous music man never made
        As sight and sound's adornment there.

9   So all was adorned in a wonderful way.
    The forest where Fortune drew me forth
    Showed such splendours that none could say
    With telling by tongue their true worth.
    And still I blithely strode that strand,
    No slope so steep as to cause me stay.
    Ahead, still fairer was the forest land:
    Plant and spice and pear-tree gay,
        Hedge and border and bright mead lay
        On banks as brilliant as threads of gold,
        Between which the water cut its way –
        Lord, most truly, adornment untold!

10 The adornments of that wonderful deep
    Were banks of beryl that lambent shone;
    Sweetly swirling was the water's sweep
    As whisperingly it wandered on.

Dazzling stones shone in the deep
Like glint through glass, glowing and bright;
As streaming stars, when dalesmen sleep,
Flare in the welkin on winter night.
    For every stone that met my sight
    Was emerald, sapphire or other gem,
    So that all the water gleamed with light
    In the gracious adornment given by them.

III

11 The precious adornment of down and dale,
    Of wood and water and noble plain,
    Brought me to bliss, made bitterness fail,
    Allayed my distress, destroyed my pain.
    Down by a stream of steady flow
    I moved in bliss, my mind a-thrill,
    And further along that river-land low,
    The joy of my heart grew stronger still.
        As Fortune grants us good or ill,
        Sending solace or sorrow sore,
        The man on whom she works her will
        May have of his lot more and more.

12 Yet more the blessings abounding there
    Than I could tell in endless leisure,
    For earthly heart could scarcely bear
    A tenth part of that precious pleasure.
    And so it seemed that Paradise
    Beyond those spacious slopes was displayed;
    That, severing the joys, a water device
    With connecting pools had been neatly made.
        Beyond the water, by hill or glade,
        The moated castle bounds must be.
        But the water was deep; I dared not wade,
        Though longing yet more was luring me.

13 More and more, and yet still more,
    Beyond the brook I longed to explore,
    For fair though the form of the hither shore,
    More beauty still the further bore.
    Stumbling, I searched about the land
    To find a way to ford the mere,
    But the farther I strode along the strand,
    The more, I thought, perils might appear.

Yet still it seemed I should not fear,
And turn my back on such a store
Of things unheard-of thronging near,
And moving my mind more and more.

14 More marvels yet daunted my mind;
I saw beyond that blissful stream
A glittering cliff of crystal kind,
Ablaze with many a kingly beam.
At its foot a girl sat, gracious sight,
A noble maiden most debonair
In garments all of glistening white,
And known to me well, before, elsewhere.
Like glittering gold refined with care,
So shone that glory above the shore:
Long I looked upon her there,
And gazing, knew her more and more.

15 The more I scanned her seemly face,
When I had found her form so fair,
The more I was suffused apace
By glorious gladness gliding there.
I longed to call her, but then a daze,
A numb surprise through my spirit spread
At seeing her in so strange a place:
My soul was struck with a sudden dread.
But then she lifted her lovely head,
With face as white as ivory pure.
It stabbed my heart, struck it with dread,
And ever the longer, the more and more.

IV

16 More than it pleased me, my dread arose:
Stock still I stood, and dared not call.
With open eyes, and mouth shut close,
I stood as gentle as hawk in hall.
I thought that vision a ghostly shade,
And greatly feared what might befall,
Lest she I saw should from me fade,
And I not hold her close at all.
And then that maiden, so slight, so small,
That flawless and most gracious girl,
Arose in garb majestical,
A precious piece all set in pearl.

17   A set of pearls for princely use
A mortal might by grace have seen
When the maiden, fresh as flower-de-luce,
Came swiftly stepping down the dean.
Gleaming white was her garb of lawn,
With open sides, and the trimmings were
With loveliest pearls more prettily borne
Than any my eyes had beheld, I swear.
   The falling sleeves, of ample flare,
   Were adorned with double pearly gems;
   In matching mode, her skirt was fair,
   With precious pearls set in its hems.

18   Set in the crown on the head of that girl
Was margarite only, no other stone;
High pinnacled was the pure white pearl,
With figured flowers worked thereon.
No other circlet was on her hair,
Which hung all round her, loosely thrown.
As duke's, or earl's, grave was her air,
And her skin was whiter than whalebone.
   Like sheer cut gold her tresses shone,
   And lay on her shoulders, light and unbound.
   Her marvellous whiteness matched that upon
   The pearly embroidery set around.

19   Set were the cuffs and hems each one
With silvery pearl, no other stone,
At hands, at sides, at openings shown;
And burnished white her vesture shone.
But a pearl unblemished, a priceless treasure,
Was firmly fastened upon her breast:
Before man's mind could find its measure,
His power of thought would be much oppressed.
   No tongue to its beauty could well attest,
   Or figure it forth in fitting phrase,
   Such perfect purity it possessed,
   That precious pearl so set in its place.

20   Set in pearls, that precious piece
Down the slope began to glide:
No gladder man from here to Greece
Than I when she stood on the stream's side!

Being nearer than aunt or niece in birth,
She won me to a yet gladder way.
She proffered me speech, best creature on earth,
Inclining low as a maiden may,
    Took off her crown of costly array,
    And gladly greeted me, gracious girl.
    Ah, bliss to be born for such a day,
    To answer that sweet one set in pearl!

V

21   'O Pearl,' I said, 'with pearls so strown,
Are you my margarite whom I have mourned,
Night-long lamented, all alone?
For you in suffering I have yearned,
Since in the grass you slipped from sight.
In throes of thought I dwell most dread,
But you have lit on a life of delight
In Paradise, free from strife and fear.
    What fate has conveyed my jewel here,
    But dealt me grief and dangers keen?
    Since we were severed and sundered in sphere,
    A joyless jeweller have I been.'

22   That jewel then, so begemmed a girl,
Looked up, most lovely and grey of eye,
Put on her crown of orient pearl,
And gravely gave me this reply:
'Sir, not fitly have you professed
Your Pearl completely cast away,
When she is enclosed in a coffer blest,
This garden here, gracious and gay,
    Herein to dwell for ever and play,
    Where comes not grief, or loss, or care.
    For certain, here were your casket, I say,
    If you were a jeweller fair.

23   'But, gentle jeweller, if you must lose
Your joy for a gem you held so dear,
You care for a cause which quickly goes –
You are fixed in folly, it would appear.
For what you miss is a mere rose,
Which flowered and faded as Nature knows;
But through the casket which keeps it close,
A pearl of price has come from that rose.

Your fate is a thief, you falsely gloze,
When gain from nothing it gave to you.
You blame the balsam of your woes:
No gentle jeweller would so do.'

24 A jewel to me then was this gentle guest,
And jewels her gentle words, no less.
I said, 'Most blissful one and best,
You drive away my dire distress.
To be excused I make request.
I thought my Pearl was thrust from the light,
But she is found, and I so blest
Shall dwell with her in the woodlands bright,
    And praise my Lord and his laws aright
    For bringing this bliss so close to me.
    Beyond these waves with my maiden white,
    A joyful jeweller could I be.'

25 'Jeweller,' said that gem so clear,
'Why do you jest so witlessly?
Three words at once you have uttered here,
And ill-advised were all the three.
You know not what in the world they mean,
So far in front of your wit they flee.
You assert my existence in this dean,
Because my form you fairly see;
    You say besides that here with me
    You mean to remain; you thirdly say
    You will cross this flowing water free,
    And that, no joyful jeweller may.

VI

26 'I judge that jeweller unworthy of praise
Who wholly believes what he sees with his eye,
And greatly to blame and bare of grace
He who believes Our Lord could lie.
Your life he swore to exalt and guide,
Though Fate condemned your flesh to die;
Yet, crediting only what can be eyed,
You rashly read his words awry.
    And pride it is, none can deny,
    A vice no virtuous man should show,
    When to no tale's truth you testify,
    Unless mere logic judge of it so.

27 'Now judge if justly you complain,
As a man to God making lament.
You mean to dwell in this domain,
But first you ought to seek his consent,
A quest in which you well might fail.
You wish to cross this waterway,
But wait till other words prevail:
Your corpse most cold must sink to clay,
 Doomed in Paradise to due decay
 When Adam soiled it: to cross this stream,
 Through death must man first drive his way,
 And then be let pass by the Judge Supreme.'

28 'You adjudge me then, my sweet,' said I,
'To grief again? Then I waste away.
Must I so lose before I die
What, lost so long, I found today?
So robbed, so rallied, what fate is mine?
My precious Pearl assigns me pain.
To what end wealth but to make men pine,
When loss of it brings bitter bane?
 I shall never heed now if my welfare wane,
 Or I am flung from the fold of men:
 And thus deprived of my Pearl again,
 What but long woe shall men judge it then?'

29 'You judge the stress of sorrow alone,'
The girl then said. 'Why do you so?
Men greeting minor griefs with groan
Miss mightier matters when they show.
But you should cross yourself instead,
And ever love God, in weal and woe,
For grief will gain you not a shred.
Be meek, for sufferings man must know.
 And though you toss like a trapped doe,
 Thrashing in throe with wild screams,
 And fare no further, to or fro,
 You are bound to bear what your Judge deems.

30 'Judge God for ever, arraign, indict,
He will not waver an inch from the way.
Your gains will mount by not one mite,
Though grieving so, you never be gay.

So check your wrangling, your chiding close,
And swiftly seek his mercy's sight;
Plead for that mercy to interpose
And manifest its marvellous might.
  His comfort can end your anguished plight
  With ease; and whether your agonies
  Are hidden or wailed in the open light,
  Yet in every case, judgement is his.'

VII

31 Her judgement then thus answered I:
  'Let my Lord not find it an offence
  If stumbling in speech I rashly cry;
  My heart, so hurt with loss intense,
  Streams out sorrow like a spring in spate.
  I always lean on the mercy of the Lord.
  Never rebuke me in cruel debate,
  However I blunder, my dear adored.
    Your kindly comfort to me afford,
    In pitying thought pondering this:
    Between care and me you made accord,
    You, ever the ground of all my bliss.

32 'My bliss, my bane! You have been both,
  But greater than them my grief, alas!
  Since you were snatched from snares on earth,
  Never have I known where my Pearl was.
  But now I see her, my grief is gone.
  At the time of parting we were at one:
  God forbid our bond be undone,
  For we seldom meet by stump or stone.
    Although your talk is courtly in tone,
    I am but dust, my manners are amiss:
    But the mercy of Christ, and Mary and John,
    Are ever the ground of all my bliss.

33 'In bliss I see you blithely set,
  And I cast down in depth of woe;
  But little thought you give to that,
  Though searing sorrows I often know.

I beg you, now that I am here,
To tell me, barring all debate,
In solemn concord and statement clear,
What life you lead early and late.
 I rejoice to know that now your fate
 Is happy and honoured, as seems by this.
 That thought holds me in high estate
 And is ever the ground of all my bliss.'

34 'May bliss befall you, sir,' she replied,
Lovely of limb and fair of face,
'And welcome here to walk and bide,
For now your words have won my grace.
Masterful temper and towering pride,
I tell you, are truly hated here.
My Lord is loath to rebuke or chide,
For all are meek who stay in his sphere.
 When in his presence you appear,
 Be humble therefore, and wholly devout.
 My Lord the Lamb ever loves such cheer,
 He, my ground of bliss throughout.

35 'A blissful life you say I lead:
Learn how I rose to it stage by stage.
When your Pearl was taken, you knew indeed
How young I was, of what tender age.
But my Lord the Lamb, being divine,
Made me his with marriage pledge,
Crowned me queen, in bliss to shine,
And gain a growing privilege.
 Thus dowered with all his heritage
 Is his love: I am wholly his.
 His praise, his worth and lineage
 Are root and ground of all my bliss.'

VIII

36 'My bliss, how can that be?' said I.
'Be not offended if I am at fault,
But can you be Queen of the azure sky,
Whom all creation should exalt?

We believe in Mary, matchless in grace,
Who bore a babe from her virgin-flower.
Her queenly crown who could displace
But one who surpassed her worth and power?
    Now for her sweetness, uniquely pure,
    We call her Phoenix of Araby,
    Which flew from its Maker, faultless and sure,
    Much like the Queen of Courtesy.'

37 'Ah, courteous Queen!' the fair one said,
Kneeling low, and lifting her face.
'Matchless Mother, most joyful Maid,
Blessed Beginner of every grace!'
Then up she rose and after a pause
Gave me her gentle speech again:
'Sir, many here venture and win their cause,
But no usurpers do we sustain.
    In heaven this Empress has her reign,
    And earth and hell besides has she:
    Yet none shall dismiss her from her domain,
    For she is the Queen of Courtesy.

38 'The court of the kingdom of God alive
Has a virtue self-distinguishing:
For every one of all who arrive
Of the whole realm is queen or king;
And yet no other shall he deprive,
But rejoice in others' inheriting,
Wishing each crown the worth of five,
Could betterment profit so pure a thing.
    But my Lady, Jesu's fountain-spring,
    Over us all holds empery:
    Which annoys none of our gathering,
    For she is the Queen of Courtesy.

39 'In courtesy, Saint Paul has said
We all are members of Jesus Christ.
For leg and navel, arm and head,
Are true parts of the body comprised.
Just so each Christian soul belongs
As limb to the Lord of spiritual light.
So think what rancours or hateful wrongs
Between your limbs are fastened tight.

The head feels neither resentment nor spite
At arm's or finger's flaunted ring.
So live we all in love and delight
Through Courtesy to our Queen and King.'

40 'Courtesy,' I said, 'I believe,
And great charity, thrive in your throng,
But – and may I not make you grieve –
What else you say seems sadly wrong.
Yourself too high in heaven you heave
To call yourself queen, having been so young.
What higher honour could man achieve,
Suffering on earth, steadfast and strong,
    Living in penance his whole life long
    And buying his bliss with his agony?
    What greater glory to him could belong
    Than crowning him king through courtesy?

IX

41 'That courtesy has too free a hand
If truth it is that now you say.
A bare two years you lived in our land,
Could not gratify God or pray;
Paternoster, Creed, you never knew –
Yet called to queenship the first day!
I cannot credit, God bless me true,
That God could go so greatly astray.
    To the state of countess in heaven, say,
    God might a maiden like you appoint,
    Or that of lady of lesser sway;
    But queen! that comes to too high a point.'

42 'No point too high for his bounty can be,'
Then said to me that maiden bright,
'For only truth can he decree,
And he does nothing but what is right.
As Matthew in your mass makes clear,
Quoting God in his gospel true,
In parable he can pose an idea,
And shew it as shining heaven to the view.
    "My lofty kingdom I liken to
    A lord," he said, "with a vine estate.
    As the year turned, the time was due
    To work the vines on the appointed date.

43   ' "This appointed date was known to all,
And the lord rose early to hire the hands
To work the vineyard, and at his call
Came men to labour his commands.
Forth to the fields they working went,
Contracted to toil for a penny a day;
Cutting and pruning with sturdy intent,
And tying the sprigs that went astray.
    To market, later, the lord made his way,
    And finding there many an idle man,
    Asked them, 'What, not working today?
    Has this day no appointed plan?'

44   ' " 'By point of day,' they replied as one,
'We were waiting here for work, on call,
But none since we saw the morning sun
Has offered us any work at all.'
'Go to my vineyard, do what you can.'
So said the lord, and clinched their consent.
'And what by evening is owing to a man,
I truly shall pay him, in deed and intent.'
    So into the vineyard to work they went.
    Meanwhile the lord thus went his way,
    And fresh workers to the vineyard sent,
    Almost till the ending point of day.

45   ' "At the point of day for evensong,
An hour before the set of the sun,
He saw there idlers, fit and strong,
And spoke to them in serious tone:
'Why do you idle this whole day long?'
They had had no offers of work, said they.
'Go to my vineyards, yeomen young,
And work mightily, as best you may.'
    Soon on the land the darkness lay;
    The sun had set and it became late.
    He summoned the men to receive their **pay;**
    The day was done, the appointed date.

X

46   ' "This point the lord observed and so
He said to his steward, 'Pay the hands.
Pay them the hire I fairly owe,
And further, that none may fault my commands,

Set them all in a single row
And give each man his penny gain.
Work from the last man standing low,
Till you reach the first at the front of the train.'
  The first came forward, began to complain
  That their toil had made them tired and sore:
  'These but an hour have stood the strain;
  In money we ought to be paid much more.

47 ' " 'More have we served, we reckon so,
Bearing the heat of the whole day thus,
Than these who have toiled but an hour or two:
But yet you liken them to us.'
Then said the lord to one of these,
'No cut in your contract, friend, I moot,
So pocket your due and depart in peace.
For a penny you all accepted my suit,
  Each one of you, so why dispute?
  Having firmly agreed on a penny before,
  To plead beyond it brings no repute:
  How then ought you to ask for more?

48 ' " 'And more, is giving of my own free will
Not granted lawful when I give my own?
Or does your eye see only ill
In my being fair, and false to none?'
Christ said, 'I shall arrange it so:
The last shall be first his pay to collect,
And the first, though fleet, shall be last to go:
For many are called, but few the elect.' "
  The portion of the poor none shall neglect,
  Though late they come, and live obscure.
  Their labour having so little effect,
  God's mercy is by so much the more.

49 'More bliss and joy I have herein,
Through perfect life and ladyship great,
Than anyone in the world might win
By claiming fair reward from Fate.
Yet hardly had I started forth –
At dusk to the vines I made my way –
But my Lord at once knew my labour's worth,
And paid me in full without delay.

Yet others came early, spent the whole day,
Laboured and sweated long and sore,
And notwithstanding received no pay,
And may not for a year or more.'

50 Then more and plainly I spoke my mind:
'Your reasoning seems to me unstable.
Instant and right is the rule divine,
Else Holy Writ is only a fable.
The Psalmist openly asserts,
In a verse whose words that sense convey:
"You grant to each his true deserts,
O ordinant King of endless sway."
      The steadfast man who strove all day
      Saw you win your reward before:
      So the less the work, the more the pay,
      And so on for ever, more and more.'

XI

51 'Between the more and less in heaven,'
Said the courteous one, 'All is accord,
For similar hire to each is given,
Whether great or small his right reward.
No grudging giver is our Chieftain great,
Be his judgement gentle or hard;
He pours his gifts like a gully in spate,
Or stream from source which none can retard.
      Much gain is his who has regard
      For him who saves us from sinful deed:
      From bliss he never shall be debarred,
      For the grace of God is enough indeed.

52 'Enough that you argue, to do me shame,
I have had my penny wrongly here.
You say that because too late I came,
I ought not to move in so high a sphere.
When did you know a man of use
So steadfast in holy prayer austere,
That he did not sometime stand to lose
The high reward of heaven so clear?
      And ever more often, the older they were,
      The more they abandoned right for wrong.
      Mercy and grace then must give them care;
      And the grace of God is enough and strong.

53 'But grace enough have the innocent.
No sooner born but in steady lines
To baptismal water they make descent;
Then are they brought to work the vines,
And suddenly day, with darkness blent,
To the night of death declines and falls.
Those free from sin before they went,
The high Lord pays as his own thralls.
    They lived on earth, they came at his call:
    Why should he not give work its due,
    Yes, fully and forthwith pay them all?
    God's grace is great enough so to do.

54 'Well enough it is known that noble man
Was fashioned at first for bliss in the height,
Which bliss for Adam came under ban
Through an apple of which he had a bite.
That food has damned us all to dwell
And die lamenting far from delight,
And after to go to hottest hell,
And live there long without respite.
    But quickly a cure for this came to light:
    On cruel Cross the rich blood ran,
    And precious water: then in that plight
    God's grace grew great enough for man.

55 'Enough indeed washed from that well,
Water and blood from the wound so wide:
The blood brought us from bane of hell
And stopped our second death being died.
The water is baptism, truth to tell,
Which followed the spear so grimly ground,
And washes away the guilts which fell
From Adam so that in death we drowned.
    Between us and bliss the whole world round
    There is nothing now God has not cast off.
    To bliss once more we are blessedly bound,
    And the grace of God is great enough.

XII

56 'Grace enough a man may gain
If freshly falling to sin, he pray,
But he must beseech it in spiritual pain,
And the whole penalty for sin must pay.

But reason must ever true right sustain
And spare the innocent every day.
God never appointed in judgement plain
That harm should come the innocent's way.
  The guilty, through contrition, may
  With mercy in God's true grace abide,
  But, never wandering evil's way,
  The innocent are saved and justified.

57 'Just so I assert that in this case
It is right to save two by reason's skill.
The just man shall view God's face,
And the innocent also shall gaze his fill.
A passage in Psalms puts it in phrase:
"Lord, who shall climb thy lofty hill,
Or stay within thy holy place?"
He answers himself with eager will:
  "He whose hands have done no ill,
  Whose heart is wholly clean and pure,
  Shall set his foot there, steadfast and still."
  So are the innocent justly sure.

58 'The just, so Scripture judges wholly,
Who trick no neighbours with treacherous guile,
And do not profane their lives with folly,
Shall approach that fairest fortress pile.
Of such Solomon has clearly said
That Wisdom won them honoured gain.
By straightest ways their steps she led
To show them awhile where God holds reign,
  As saying, "Mark that fair domain!
  You can win it by resolute will."
  But certainly, without peril or pain,
  The innocent are saved by justice still.

59 'To the just besides, if you saw it somewhere,
This saying the Psalmist David applied:
"Lord, never take thy servant to trial,
For to thee none living is justified."
Therefore when you come to the court
Where all our cases ought to be tried,
And count on justice, expect to be caught
By this same speech that I have spied.

But he who bled on the Cross and died,
Pitifully pierced through both his hands,
May yield you passage when you are tried
For your innocence, not your just demands.

60 'He who justly reads can behold
The holy book and see displayed
How Jesus walked among folk of old,
Who hurried their offspring to him for aid
From the health and favour he emanated.
That he would touch them, they earnestly prayed.
These suppliants then his disciples frustrated,
And by their disputing many were stayed.
　　Then to them Jesus sweetly said,
　　"Let these little ones come unto me,
　　For of such is the Kingdom of Heaven made".
　　The innocent are saved by the just plea.[1]

XIII

61 'To his gentle ones then Jesus mild
Called, saying none to his kingdom could win
Unless he came there like a child;
No other way could he enter in.
When the innocent, undefiled in grace,
Without stain or spot of polluting sin,
Knock for entrance to the holy place,
Promptly shall men the portal unpin.
　　There bliss abiding has ever been,
　　Which with gems the jeweller sought;
　　Sold all his wealth, both wool and linen,
　　To buy himself a pearl without spot.

62 'This spotless pearl, purchased so dear,
For which the jeweller gave his goods,
Is like the kingdom of heaven clear,
So said the Father of field and flood;
For it is pure, of taintless worth,
A perfect round, transparent-hued,
And belongs to all who were just on earth;
Lo, in the middle of my breast it stood.

1. There is no link-word concatenating this stanza with the following one.
Professor Gordon suggests that a scribal error is responsible for this unique
failure.

My Lord the Lamb, who shed his blood,
Placed it there as peaceful pledge.
Forsake this world with its savage mood,
And purchase this pearl, your spotless wage!'

63 'O spotless Pearl in pure pearls placed,
Bearing,' said I, 'the pearl of price,
Who framed your form so fairly graced?
He who worked your clothes was wise.
Your beauty never came of Nature:
Pygmalion could never your painter be,
Nor could Aristotle ever feature
In science your kind of quality.
 O fairer than the fleur-de-lys,
 With angel-having, gracious girl,
 Tell me, bright one, what great degree
 Bears as badge so spotless a pearl?'

64 'My spotless Lamb who turns all to grace,'
Said she, 'my darling destiny,
Made me his mate, though out of place
That union once appeared to be.
When I went from the world's wet weather,
To his beatitude he summoned me,
Saying, "My sweet beloved, come hither,
For in you no spot or stain do I see,"
 Beauty and might he gave to me,
 Bathed my clothes in blood on the dais,
 Crowned me clean in virginity,
 And dressed me in pearl, spotless in grace.'

65 'O spotless bride, as bright as flame,
Rich in titles and royal life,
What sort of Lamb can be this same
To want you as his wedded wife?
So high you climb above all the rest
To live with him in lady-like sway;
Yet many a beauty brightly tressed
Has struggled for Christ a weary way.
 And all those dear ones you drove away
 From marriage with him, all, all forgot
 Except yourself, bold in the fray,
 A matchless maiden without a spot.'

XIV

66   'Spotless,' said that comely queen,
    'Unblemished I am, without a blot;
    That I can claim with courteous mien,
    But "matchless queen" then said I not.
    Wives of the Lamb are we in bliss,
    A hundred and forty-four thousand blest,
    As it appears in the Apocalypse:
    Saint John beheld their throng addressed
      On Zion's stately mountain crest;
      The Apostle saw them in a spirit dream
      Adorned on the hilltop, for marriage dressed,
      In the city of the New Jerusalem.

67   'This I relate of Jerusalem:
    If you would know of what kind he is,
    My Lamb, my Lord, my darling gem,
    My fair beloved, my joy, my bliss,
    The words of Isaiah the prophet ran
    On his meekness most compassionately:
    "Glorious, guiltless, yet killed by man,
    Though from fault and felony free;
      Led as a lamb to the slaughter was he;
      Like a sheep held fast when the shearer came,
      He closed his lips to every plea
      When the Jews judged him in Jerusalem."

68   'In Jerusalem my beloved was slain,
    And rent on the Cross by ruffians bold:
    Willing to bear our woes and pain,
    He took to himself our sorrows untold.
    His face, so fine to see and fair,
    They lashed and flayed without restraint;
    For all our sin he had the care,
    He whom sin could never taint.
      He let himself be scourged, constrained
      And stretched on a crude, massive beam,
      Where meek as a lamb, without complaint,
      He died for us in Jerusalem.

69   'In Jerusalem, Jordan, and Galilee,
    Baptism was given by good Saint John,
    Whose words with those of Isaiah agree.
    When Jesus came towards him, John

Uttered of him this prophecy:
"Lo! God's Lamb, rock-firm, alone,
Of all our evils he makes us free,
And salves the sins that man has done.
    Though he himself committed none,
    To all of man's he makes his claim.
    Who can tell the line of the One
    Who died for us in Jerusalem?"

70 'In Jerusalem thus my darling love,
By true witness of two prophets there,
Was taken for a lamb in token of
His gentle mind and modest cheer.
The third time, which these two approve,
Appears in the Apocalypse written clear.
Enthroned in the midst of the saints above,
John the Apostle saw him there,
    Opening the book with the pages square,
    And seven seals on the cover seam;
    And hosts, beholding, quake in fear,
    In hell, on earth, in Jerusalem.

XV

71 'This Jerusalem Lamb was free from blot
Of any hue but brilliant white,
On which could stay no stain or spot,
The wool was so abundant and white.
So every soul unsullied by wrong
Makes for the Lamb a worthy wife,
And though each day his new brides throng,
Among us rises no wrangling or strife.
    We wish indeed each one were five –
    The more the merrier, if such God bless.
    Our mighty musters make our love thrive
    In ever more honour, and never less.

72 'And less of bliss no man can bring
To us who bear pearl upon the breast,
For they never think of quarrelling
Who carry a spotless pearl as crest.
Although our bodies to ground have gone
Decaying – and this you cry without rest –
To the final wisdom we have won,
Our faith in One Death manifest:

Our cares banished, by the Lamb blest,
Who makes all glad at every mass,
The bliss of each one supremely best:
No honour unique, but never less.

73   'Lest to believe me you do not incline,
See in Apocalypse a passage there.
"I saw," says John, "on the Mount of Zion,
The Lamb standing, exalted and fair,
And a hundred thousand virgins arrayed,
And four and forty thousand more,
All with him there, and every head
The names of the Lamb and the Father bore.
    I heard then a shout from the heaven I saw:
    Than voice of turbulent torrents' stress,
    Or thunder in throes on a black tor,
    That sound, I believe, was never less.

74   ' "Nevertheless, though loud the shout
And the swell of sound with their voices' might,
I heard a new song chanted out,
To listen to which was pure delight.
As clear as harp-notes that harpists play,
The strains of their sounding music were,
Gently toned in a wonderful way,
As sweetly together they sang the air.
    In front of God the Father's chair,
    And the Elders in their stateliness,
    And the four beasts that bow to him there,
    They sang their song never the less.

75   ' "Nevertheless none have skill so strong,
For all the arts that ever they knew,
To sing one strain of that heavenly song,
Except the True Lamb's retinue;
For they are purged of earth, appointed
As first-fruits to God most fully due,
And join the gentle Lamb, his anointed,
Being like himself in speech and hue.
    For never did lying or tale untrue
    Touch their tongues through evil stress;
    And never shall part that pure retinue
    From their Master immaculate, nevertheless." '

76 'Not less let my thanks be thought,' said I,
'Although on my Pearl I press surmise.
Your noble wit I should not try,
You, chosen for the chamber of Christ.
I am but mingled dust and mire,
But you, fresh rose of richness intense,
Abide on this bank of bliss entire
Among eternal living contents.
    Now, gracious one girdled in innocence,
    I would put to you a point express,
    And though I seem stupid and thick in sense,
    Let my suit stand nevertheless.

XVI

77 'Nevertheless clearly to you I call,
If you will deign that this be done:
As you are glorious and free from fault,
Never deny me my piteous boon.
Have you no home within castle-wall,
No dwelling, no meeting-place of your own?
You tell of Jerusalem, realm most royal,
Adorned with kingly David's throne.
    Not in these woods, but Judea, the zone
    Must be of that citadel noble of note.
    Maid most immaculate under the moon,
    Your abode is bound to be without mote.'

78 'This moteless multitude, mighty throng
Of many thousands mentioned by you,
Must surely possess a city strong
To hold so huge a retinue?
So comely a cluster of jewels fair
Were evilly housed, having no home;
But I see no building anywhere
Beside these beautiful banks I roam.
    Do you not walk here, lingering alone
    To look on this glorious stream of note?
    If you possess a castle home,
    Show me the way to its well-made moat.'

79 'The moated place which you mean in Judea,'
Replied that girl of fragrance refined,
'Is the city sought by the Lamb so dear
To suffer in sorely for all mankind –

The old Jerusalem, we rightly deem,
Where the first sin had its final check.
But in the Apocalypse the apostle's theme
Was the new city, brought by God's own beck.
 The Lamb, unblackened by a single speck,
 Has conveyed there his fairest company,
 A flock entirely without fleck,
 Like his city, from all mote free.

80 'Of moated cities we mention two,
Both named Jerusalem nevertheless,
Which well may mean no more to you
Than "City of God" or "Sight of Peace".[1]
In the one our peace was established well:
The Lamb picked it for his pain and wrong.
In the other only peace can dwell,
And shall, through endless ages long.
 That is the city to which we throng
 When flesh is laid in grave to rot,
 Where honour and bliss grow ever more strong
 For the multitude unblemished by mote.'

81 'Moteless maiden so meek and mild,'
Then said I to that fairest flower,
'Bring me to that bountiful pile
And let me see your blissful bower.'
'God will forbid it,' the bright one said.
'You shall not enter his holy place
Until the Lamb I may persuade
To grant you a sight of it through his grace.
 Upon that precinct pure you may gaze
 From outside, but in it set no foot.
 You have no power to walk its ways,
 Unless you are pure and without mote.

XVII

82 'To this moated place let me be guide:
Walk up towards the head of this rill,
And I shall follow on this opposite side,
Until your path takes you uphill.'

1. Jerusalem in Hebrew means, 'They shall see peace'.

Then, staying not, I brushed aside
The bright-leafed boughs in my ascent,
Until from the top of a hill I spied
Beyond the brook, as onward I went,
 The Celestial City in slow descent:
 And brighter than beaming sun it shone.
 The Apocalypse makes plain the event,
 Put in words of the Apostle John.

83 As John the Apostle the sight surveyed,
 I saw that city of noble renown,
 The New Jerusalem, royally arrayed,
 From heaven on high floating down.
 Like polished glass, in glittering gleams
 The fire-bright gold of the city reared,
 And underneath it were noble gems.
 The fixed foundations were twelve times tiered,
  And each course with the next cohered,
  Though made of a separate precious stone;
  Just as the city superbly appeared
  In the Apocalypse of the Apostle John.

84 As John to each of these jewels gave name,
 I reckon each stone from his narration.
 Jasper was the name of the first gem
 I saw adorning the base foundation;
 It glimmered green on the lowest tier.
 On the second step, sapphire was seen,
 Then chalcedony, stainless and clear,
 On the third step showed with pallid sheen.
  The fourth was emerald with hue of green;
  The sardonyx was the fifth stone,
  And the sixth was ruby, as it was seen
  In the Apocalypse, by the Apostle John.

85 And John yet counted the chrysolite,
 The seventh stone on the tiered plinth.
 The eighth was beryl, clear and white,
 And topaz inlaid with twin hues ninth;
 The tenth, chrysoprase, firmly fixed,
 And gentle jacinth the eleventh stone.
 The purple and indigo amethyst,
 Cure of all woes, made the twelfth zone.

Above these bases, the wall was done
In jasper; like shining glass it shone.
I knew it, shaped and hued as shown
In the Apocalypse, by the Apostle John.

86 As John described it, I saw it there.
Broad and deep was the twelve-tiered stair,
And the city reared above it square,
In length and breadth and height most fair.
The golden streets shone clear as glass;
The wall of jasper glinted like glair;[1]
The mansions within were bright with a mass
Of precious jewels beyond compare.
This princely palace's every square
In length and breadth and height was shown
To be twelve furlongs, as measured there
By judgement of the Apostle John.

XVIII

87 Of John's vision I viewed yet more:
Each side of the city had three gates
– Twelve on the towering exterior I saw –
The portals adorned with rich metal plates,
Each gate composed of pearl the same,
That pearl whose purity never abates.
And borne by each gate was the Bible name
Of a tribe of Israel, in order of dates,
As the birth-fortune prognosticates.[2]
The eldest was the first to be hewn.
There gleamed such light in all the streets,
They needed neither sun nor moon.

88 Of sun and moon they had no need,
For the Very God was their lamp of light,
And the Lamb of God was their lantern indeed,
Through whom the whole of the city shone bright.

1. White of egg, as used in illumination of manuscripts, etc. (Gordon).
2. An echo of Exodus xxviii, 10. The description there of the High Priest's ephod, and the description of the New Jerusalem in Revelation, became associated with each other because of the similarity between the two lists of precious stones.

My gaze went through wall and dwelling,
Transparency letting pass all light,
And there, in splendour all excelling,
You might behold the enthroned height,
    As John the Apostle pictured it right,
    With God himself seated thereon.
    Straight from the throne ran a river bright,
    More brilliant than both the sun and moon.

89   Sun and moon never shone so sweet
As that river flowing forth from the floor.
Swiftly it swept through every street;
No filth or slime or sludge it bore.
No church or chapel or temple was there:
The Almighty was their minister great;
The Lamb, the sacrifice most fair,
Was present their souls to resuscitate.
    At every roadway, the entrance gate
    Was evermore open, late and soon;
    Yet none could enter whose estate
    Bore a blemish beneath the moon.

90   The moon can draw therefrom no might;
Too spotty she is, of body too grim:
Besides, the city never has night.
Why should the moon her circuit swim
And labour to match the marvellous light
That beams on that noble water's brim?
The planets are in too poor a plight,
And the sun itself by far too dim.
    Quickly the brilliant trees by the stream
    Bring forth twelve fruits of life in bloom:
    Twelve times with richest fruit they teem,
    Freshly reviving with every moon.

91   Under the moon a miracle so great
As this my seeing that citadel wall
Would kill a man of mortal state,
So marvellous was the making of all.
I stood as still as a startled quail,
Astonished at that stately sight.
Stillness and stir: I felt both fail,
So ravished was I by its radiance bright.

With conscience clear I saw outright
That mortal body beholding that boon,
Though priests in plenty tended his plight,
Would lose all light beneath the moon.

XIX

92 As the moon in might makes its rise
Before the gleams of day all go,
So suddenly in wonderful wise
I sensed a procession of stately show.
This glorious city, august in fame,
Was suddenly, without summoning sound,
Full of such maidens, clothed the same,
As my own beloved, blissful and crowned.
    So crowned were they all, so gowned,
    So pearl-apparelled, and all in white,
    And steadfast on every bosom bound
    Was the blissful pearl of great delight.

93 Great their delight as gliding they came
By golden ways that gleamed like glass,
All together, their garments the same.
It were hard to find the happiest face
In all that hundred thousand, I hold.
Proudly the Lamb, in foremost place,
With the seven horns of pure red gold,
In pearl-like robes, set a solemn pace.
    These many, not jostling, but justly spaced,
    Thronged in array to the throne of light,
    Like maidens to mass, mildly, with grace,
    So moving, so advancing with much delight.

94 Delight that the Lamb had come to the dais
Was much too great for a man to tell:
The Elders, as he approached the place,
Before his feet prostrate fell.
Angels in concourse, together called,
Scattered incense of sweetest smell.
All, to praise of that Jewel enthralled,
Sang glory and joy in a new song's swell.
    Their sound could strike through earth to hell,
    When the Virtues of Heaven voice their delight.
    To worship the Lamb as those who dwell
    On high with him seemed utter delight.

95 Delight in the Lamb, in looking on him,
Filled with marvel my mind amazed.
Best was he, gentlest and most to esteem
Of all the high ones I ever heard praised.
Most meek and courteous was his mien,
Although his garments were gloriously white.
But close to his heart, torn through the skin,
Was a cruel wound, bleeding and wide:
    The blood gushed out on his body's white.
    Alas, thought I, who did that spite?
    For sorrow the breast should burn up quite
    That in such torment could take delight.

96 Delight was plain in the Lamb's mien,
Despite the hurt at the wounded place;
No sign of suffering could be seen,
Such glory and gladness were in his face.
Among his multitude serene,
In overflowing life arrayed,
I looked, and beheld my little queen:
I had thought her beside me in the glade!
    Lord, what joyous music she made
    Among those maidens, she so white!
    Across the water I wished to wade,
    Moved by love-longing's great delight.

XX

97 Delight dinned in my eye and ear
And made my mortal mind give way:
Seeing my loved one, I longed to be there,
Though over the stream she had her stay.
I thought, since nothing could stop my quest
By striking a blow, or blocking my way,
I would plunge in the stream and swim the rest,
Though doing it brought my dying day.
    But as I started to go astray,
    I was sharply shaken from my design;
    From my resolve I was summoned away:
    It did not please my Prince's mind.

98 His mind demurred that I should so dash
Over magical water in frenzied fit.
Though headlong my course, eager and rash,
Yet I was swiftly stopped in it.
As I pressed to the bank at furious pace,
My frenzy made my vision fade.
I awoke in that pretty garden place:
On that selfsame hill my head was laid
    Where precious Pearl had slipped and strayed.
    I stretched and shuddered, by fear confined,
    And sighing then, to myself I said,
    'May everything pleasure my Prince's mind!'

99 Sick in mind with the sudden fright
Of being flung from that lovely place,
And every vivid, ecstatic sight,
I swooned with longing a moment's space,
Then cried in mournful, sad lament,
'O noble Pearl, of renown most dear,
Most precious to me was your argument
In this most veritable vision here.
    If you are truly, as you appear,
    To the circle of all the blessed assigned,
    I think it good, from this dungeon drear,
    That you should please that Prince's mind.'

100 If, mindful of that Prince's pleasure,
I had maintained a true intent,
And longed for only my lawful measure,
As Pearl had urged me in argument,
Most likely, sight of his mysteries
God would have granted to greater extent.
But, as for luck, man would always seize
More than makes up his complement.
    Therefore my rapture was quickly rent,
    And I cast out of the region divine.
    Lord, they are fools who fight your intent,
    Or make a move which is not to your mind.

101 Christian minds by labour light
Can please the Prince, or to peace incline;
For I have known him, by day and night,
As God, as Lord, as friend most fine.

Upon this mound I fell, so fated,
In pity for Pearl who made me pine.
So Pearl to God I dedicated,
With Christ's dear blessing and with mine.
　　May He who in form of bread and wine
　　The priest shows daily, grant we find
　　Ourselves true servants to Him Divine,
　　And precious pearls to please his mind.

The Harley Lyrics

If we did not possess the manuscript Harley 2253, from which the next twenty-two poems are taken, our knowledge of the medieval lyric at its best would be slight, and we should know next to nothing of the English courtly lyric. As with the 'Pearl' group, the lucky survival of a single manuscript both preserves precious poems, and makes us wonder what our literature may have lost by the destruction of other manuscripts. The lyrics, religious and secular, which appear on the manuscript together with other matter – Latin religious verse and prose, English fabliaux, political songs and romances, with a scattering of Anglo-Norman – seem to have been collected and written down in Herefordshire, possibly at Leominster Priory, because among the items are the lives in Latin of three local saints; but the rhymes of some of the English poems, together with other internal evidence, show that they originated in various parts of the country. The period of composition of the poems is fairly indicated by the mention in them of political events, of which the earliest took place in 1264, and the latest in 1314.

The music of the Harley Lyrics sings of a common tradition which bound priest-poet and minstrel together, however strongly they pulled away from each other. Each was aware of his rival's power over a part of the psyche proper to that rival's sphere of operation, and therefore borrowed his technique or phraseology as seemed fit. In this war of poetic interdependence, the priestly poet seems, on the whole, to have been on the defensive. His initial disadvantage, which he naturally tried to turn to advantage, was that he had to use the medium popularized by his opponent. That he knew what he was doing is made clear by the way in which, from early Christian times in Britain to Taverner and after, the Church exercised a policy of setting sacred words to the best-known popular songs.[1]

Thus the reverdie, or spring song, on the Passion, no. 81, uses the

1. Or using their melodies in some way in plainsong or anthem. Often, the intervals would be changed, and melodies developed thematically, so that the original tune might be unrecognizable to the laity.

traditional opening material of a secular love lyric like no. 85, and the *chanson d'aventure* setting of such a poem as no. 92, in which the courtly poet is a knight riding on a love-quest, may be used even when the object of 'secret love' is the Virgin Mary, as in no. 77. For his part, the poet of courtly love knows no higher terms to describe his ecstasy than those of the priest, for whom heaven is the source of all joy (the refrain of poem no. 85). But his greatest tribute to religion is that veneration of the loved one which lies at the centre of his art.

A clue to this interfusion of impulse in medieval England may be found in a decorative motif which occurs again and again in its places of worship: spring, the season of the resurrection of Christ, but also of the rebirth of nature and the upstirring of natural love, puts out its carved stone leaves on the capitals, canopies, rood-screens, roof-bosses, stalls and walls of the cathedrals. Among these leaves, which are often sufficient to themselves, may be carved such subjects as hounds chasing hares or knights killing dragons; in fact, any scenes from real or fancied life. And one common subject is the human head, often with leaves sprouting from its mouth or some other place. In poetry as in cathedral decoration, though the parts may be noted, the whole must be observed.

Of the religious lyrics appearing here, nos. 72–77 are concerned with sin and the transiency of this world, while nos. 78–82 are meditations on the Passion. Among the former are some of the finest penitential lyrics in the language.

At first reading, these poems excite wonder by their metrical elaboration, which has not been approached in the serious poetry of any other age in England. The combination of rhyme, alliteration, and link-word in such a poem as no. 73 produces a grand incantatory framework for the penitential fervour. It is as if the poet-suppliant is scourging himself with the beat and consonance in a new kind of flagellation, using verbal hammer-blows instead of whip-lashes. (The thirteenth century is the age of the Flagellants.) In poem no. 72, the same hammer-beat gives a dark and furious pomp to the denunciation of the three enemies of Man: the World, the Flesh, and the Devil. The old English epic gloom has found congenial home in a theology which turns from Woman and other joys of this life, and the writer is orthodox in terrifying his audience with hell before holding out the hope of heaven. His ignorance or disregard of the courtly values is offset by the attitude of the poet of no. 73, who, though formally repenting the sins of his courtly youth, seems to long for death not so much because it will bring him sight of the saints, as because he cannot bear life without the joys of the castle. Each value of the courtly life is listed as a sin: he had spoken 'in a seemly tone',[1] been 'held an honoured guest', had practised the 'lure of love', and had ridden in search of adventure, 'dressed for knightly deed'. He gives the lie to his own repentance by revealing, in anguished confession, that what has really driven him to despair is that he has his 'proper place no more'. Only the colouring of orthodoxy is given to his thought by the implication that God has punished him by taking away his delights; but it is not orthodox to pray for death.[2]

The poet of no. 74 achieves an intellectual acrobatic feat by justifying the courtly attitude to women in Christian terms, with a reference to the Eva-Ave antithesis (see page 24). He repents the specific sin of detraction, and in so doing exalts both the Virgin Mary and the courtly lady. The fellow-poet Richard, to whom he looks, possibly in ironic envy, is not known. In poem no. 77, the apparatus of courtly love sits more lightly on the celebration of Mary as the holy leech who can compensate us for mortal decay by giving us spiritual health.

A great concentration and purity of feeling seem to infuse the poems on the Crucifixion, which follow. Perhaps the central experience which gives meaning to Christianity would tend to exclude from poetic contemplation anything meretricious, so that when Mary is present, as in the Crucifixion Dialogue poem, no. 80, no mere conventions are allowed to occlude her function as the Mother of God. The concentration on personal reaction to Christ's suffering of poem no. 79 may be usefully contrasted with the mood of the mystery plays on the Crucifixion. Here the identification with suffering provides an elegiac commentary on the supreme dramatic moment. The injunction in the last stanza, against blasphemy, if indeed it is intended as climax, has therefore only conventional force, although its presence shows (as if demonstration were needed!) how inflexibly preoccupied with doctrine and precept the priestly poets were.

1. The power to discourse, narrate, and converse was counted a knightly grace.
2. See introduction to Poems of Sin and Death, page 60.

Carleton Brown has written a fascinating note on the companion poems no. 82 and 83, and concluded that no. 83 is the original. He notes two 'independent attempts to convert this secular song into a religious lyric', one of which praises the Virgin Mary, as one would expect, rather than Christ, as no. 82 does. Yet the priestly mind would find especial virtue in converting a song about the vicissitudes of selfish earthly love and the faithlessness of woman to one about the sacrifice and unending love of the perfect Man.

The secular poems on the Harley manuscript are not all courtly love lyrics, but they all reflect the revolution in English prosody brought about by French influence. Prosody apart, allowance must be made for the assertion of the native impulse, which, by the time these poems were written, had had two hundred years to naturalize and so change the essence of things French. To take the English poems of courtly love alone (nos. 83–91, if the wonderful poem on spring, no. 84, is correctly classified thus): they show an outlook different from that of the Provençal, or even the northern French ones. The object of love appears generally to be of the same rank as the poet, whose devotion is accordingly less servile. It has been accepted by some that the English poet addresses a '*mai*' (girl) in contrast to the '*mi dons*' (my lady) of the Provençal; but an examination of the words used in the love lyrics on the Harley manuscript does not bear this out. '*Burde*' (noble girl) and '*mai*' are used the same number of times, and the alternation of these words with '*wyf*', '*leuedi*', and '*wymman*' seems to me to be determined chiefly by metrical considerations. One must be guided by the tone of the poems, of which terminology is only one aspect. Although the poet may suffer on account of his love, no special virtue attaches to humility or 'the devotion to something afar'. But she is no peasant girl: she wears jewels and golden ornaments, is dressed in the finest linen, and can read romances (no. 86). The poet celebrates her beauty in frankly sensual terms, and woos her directly, with sharp, urgent protestation and no circumlocution: possession of her body is the aim.

At the same time, the plaintive note of a lover who seems not to expect the ultimate favour is heard, and may produce such querulous and undignified music as that of no. 91. The poet of no. 89, who at the time of writing was equally unsuccessful, dignifies his case by adding praise and honour to the girl with whom he pleads. No. 87 twists many conventional strands of *amour courtois* into its thread: despair, agony, and death are the consequence of unrequited love; the girl is discreet, generous, grey-eyed,[1] has curving brows and golden hair; her disdain for the lover does not affect his appreciation of her qualities; she is another man's wife[2]; his love is secret. Of all these writers who make unrequitedness their main theme, he of poem no. 85 is the manliest, because his stanzas, which contain the praise and the complaint, are separate from a refrain of pure joy in the fact of being in love with his Alison.

In poem no. 86, the conventional note of suffering, which is sounded twice, is scarcely heard amid the full chords of sensual enthusiasm of which the rest of the poem is composed. Hyperbole of the standard kind makes up most of the music, but suddenly the Lancashire girl's hair is let down, or the poet prefers an assignation with (or merely a sight of?) her to being Pope, and we recognize lively modulations. The ultimate charm of this rich poem lies in the humour towards the end, which shows in cynicism about the magical power of the jewel in her girdle, and in innuendo about her secret parts. Nevertheless, in this as in most elaborately rhymed and alliterated poems (but not 'Pearl'), there is a tendency for the metrical demand to prevent the best ordering of the parts of the stanza, and so to inhibit its through movement. Sometimes this metrical demand affects a whole poem, so that stanzas may become detached, and even joined to other poems, where they seem not manifestly out of place, sharing a common imagery and stanza form as they do.

Poem no. 88, which shows medieval poetic art running riot, is apt to confuse the modern reader with its cataract of similes and metaphors, no less than with its prosodical decoration. To take the stanza first: in the original, a single rhyme binds the first eight lines, and a couplet rounds it off. Each line has four stresses, and the foot is

---

1. I have read somewhere that the colour of eye then called 'grey' was in fact what we call 'blue'. The medieval poets' term seems to me more accurate than ours: they should have known, since they believed that the eye was the means by which people fell in love. Troilus, falling in love with Criseyde, is 'Right with hire look thorugh-shoten and thorugh-darted'. It followed that the blind could not fall in love.

2. The sly tilt at the commercial aspect of matrimony should warn us that irony may be found in many of these poems: sometimes it is sung with a straight face, and is therefore hard to detect.

basically anapaestic: of the fifty lines, twenty-eight are alliterated on every stress, fourteen on three of the four, and of the remaining eight lines, seven have the stresses alliterated in pairs. A bewilderingly dense ornamentation, this, which grinds the spirit with its robot-like movement. (Still, Shakespeare could perpetrate 'When first your eye I eyed'!) That apart, the plan of the poem is simple. Drawing on lapidaries, bestiaries, and herbals, whose lore would be known to all his cultured listeners, and on romance, the poet compares his girl with precious stones in the first stanza, herbs in the second, birds in the third, spices in the fourth, and heroes and heroines in the fifth.

The extent of the lore connected with each forbids detailed explanation. The importance of jewels in the Middle Ages, apart from their value, may be judged by the action of one Richard Preston, who in 1391 gave a sapphire to the shrine of Saint Erkenwald, stipulating that it should be kept 'for the cure of diseases of the eyes'. Every one of the flowers mentioned in the second stanza was highly regarded for its herbal properties: it is often unwise to distinguish between flowers and herbs when discussing plants of medieval times, because gardens usually contained nothing but herbs for use in cooking and medicine, and only the rose and the lily, potent herbs both, seem to have been cultivated for ornament. We lose something by granting only beauty to our flowers: penicillin exists in a species of moss. Most of the bird qualities are given in the third stanza, and in the fourth too, the powers of the spices are roughly indicated. Carleton Brown (*English Lyrics of the Thirteenth Century*, pp. 226–8) tries to place all the exemplars of virtue mentioned in the fifth stanza: Ragna was a wise woman, and Bjorn a hero, from Orkney saga; Tegeu was a type of chastity from Welsh Arthurian legend; Floris was the hero of a metrical romance, imprisoned by the Saracens with the Princess Blanchefleur; Craddock was an Arthurian character; the identities of Jonas and Wylcadoun have not plausibly been conjectured; Hilde was the heroine of a Germanic saga, and Garwen (if that is the correct identification for 'Wyrwein') was one of King Arthur's three mistresses, according to the Mabinogion.

As so often in medieval poetry, the catalogue of praise leads to points of sudden illumination, of which there are only two in fifty lines. The first is the pun, at the end of the third stanza, on the girl's name: in the original there was no capital letter, and the only differ-

ence between 'a note' of line 28 and 'annote' of line 29 was thus in the doubled consonant, so that the poet, though giving a clue to his lover's name, was yet keeping it secret, as the rules of courtly love required.[1] The second point of illumination is at the end, where the poet rejoices in the happy consummation of his love.

Poem no. 90 appears to be an essay in conventional morality by a man who is nevertheless eager to prove himself a courtly lover. His virtue is that he recognizes the danger to women of false adherents of the cult, who take its oaths only to dishonour them. Like the writers of no. 92 and 93, he is concerned with the lot of woman. These last two poems in the group are commonly excluded from the courtly canon on account of their popular tone, but since there is a 'perpetual ricochet between folk and courtly poetry' (Mr Hamish Henderson, of the School of Scottish Studies, University of Edinburgh, in a lecture at Aberdeen, 1962), such categorizing is of limited use. The woman's point of view is powerfully expressed in both poems: in the first, the longing for security and respectability, distrust of large promises, acceptance of fate; and in the second, cross-association of past lover with present lover, fear of relatives, warm contrariness, generation of passion by pity. A strong colloquial tone, in the near-proverbs and near-abuse which fall from the women's lips, contrasts with the courtly tone of the wooing men. These two poems tell us more of love than all the other secular Harley lyrics put together.

The poem on spring, no. 84, should charm away any tendency falsely to rationalize an aesthetic response to nature. For to feel half-dead on Saint Lucie's Day, like Donne, or amorous in May, like our poet, is proper to a beast who is, or ought to be, part of the grand harmony of nature. It is interesting to note that the outburst of spring poetry of which this poem is a part should have coincided with the period 1250–1300 which, so meteorological research tells us, probably had finer weather than England has known before or since. Such weather was deserved by people who sometimes had almost to carry out to the springing grass their surviving winter-starved cattle, which would there revive and replace the herds slaughtered and salted the previous autumn. This homage to youthful passion in the passion-tide of nature speaks for itself, and will probably seem a

1. But 'Annot' of no. 88, and 'Alison' of no. 85, may be false names concealing real or imaginary women.

perfect expression of natural impulse in spring to some man of the future, who will yet find the conventions of courtly love merely curious.

Religious Poems

72[1]

This middle-earth was made for man:
　　Its greatest gain is weak indeed;
For by the Blessed Father's plan
　　We best pay heaven highest heed:
I heard the herald of bliss appeal
　　To man to dread the Doomsday due.
The furtive felon's filthy deal
　　With secret sin shall make him spew,
　　　For though man veil the vice abhorred,
　　　And covering clothes no clue afford,
　　　Yet soul shall blaze its blots abroad.

Yes, blazed abroad this sin shall be,
　　Though sweet it seems, and soon, I say.
I put no price on pampered glee
　　Which first seems fair, then flings astray;
For loose and wicked lechery must
　　Lamenting ebb with mournful groans.
This battening on unbridled lust
　　Brings man a fate he much bemoans.
　　　At thought of thrusting on from hence,
　　　His virtue finds it foul offence
　　　To blink the closing consequence.

Until our mortal term shall close,
　　Three threaten us, and if they thrive,
They clasp the soul, those killing foes,
　　With love like loyalest men alive.
Who stands against their savage blast
　　Is blown about like bending reed:
He fears no fight who first holds fast
　　When lured to do the lecherous deed.
　　　More falsely can this foe betray
　　　Than man's five senses, so I say,
　　　For worst of all is woman's way.

1. The original stanza is twelve-lined, rhyming ababababcbcb.

Yes, woman's lust brings long despair
   If uncontrolled she riots depraved.
That devil's play shall doom the pair;
   But, saving her, man shall be saved.
By body and soul, I say as well,
   Some folk are fellowed underground
By those they hate beyond all hell.
   Bereft of bliss, the lecher bound
     In terror on earth shall trembling wait
     For bonds of pain to press him straight;
     And he shall dread a hideous fate.

Most hideous home, excepting hell,
   Is here on earth, I firmly hold;
So many foes of Man here dwell,
   And first, the Flesh, as I have told.
Next, Worldly Wealth with all its woe
   Confuses us with false delight
And goads us with its gaudy show.
   Its vicious transports vanish quite,
     And bragging, brave and overbold,
     By riches cast into the cold,
     We sicken in sin and sorrow's hold.

In sin and sorrow I am thrown;
   They dog my steps from door to door.
My mirth is mixed with grief and moan,
   Nor may I hide it any more.
Ah! Puffed in pride by wealth's delight,
   We close our ears to virtue's call.
The Devil finds us loath to fight;
   Like fading flower we rot and fall.
     Mankind's All-Father thus we flee,
     And hurled to hell that man shall be
     Who gladdens Christ in no degree.

To gladden Christ mankind was made,
   And taught to know his marvellous might.
Let none in lasting fire be flayed!
   Although we wallow in low delight,
And foemen often make us fall,
   Before our Father we shall rise,
For Christ was born to save us all.
   When trumpets summon from the skies

And God shall bid us be his own,
With righteous men we shall be shown
Standing beside the heavenly throne.

73

O God above us, grant my boon,
Maker of middle-earth and moon
    And man with mind on bliss!
True and trusty King on throne,
Reconcile my spirit soon:
    Forgive my wickedness!
Foolishly to folly prone,
In vilest vices I am thrown,
    Which harm my happiness.
I who spoke in seemly tone
Find that all my strength is flown:
    Good-bye to all my bliss!

Not blisses blear my cheeks so sore;
    I weep my wicked state.
I have my proper place no more:
People call me Clutter-Floor
    And Scoundrel Scowl-at-Grate.

While in the clasp of low delight,
In bower I was by boldest knight
    Held an honoured guest.
I fondle now no finger bright,
But loveless, only listen to slight,
    Shunned with the shabbiest.
A gout so galling grips me tight,
With many another baneful blight,
    No remedy gives me rest.
Wild as the roe I once ran light,
But now I cease that springing quite,
    By galloping gout oppressed.

On galloping horse I mounted high,
    Dressed for knightly deed;
Now beggared and bare of wealth am I—
Grief that ever I gave it eye!
    A stick is now my steed.

When I see steeds go strong in stall,
And I go halting into hall,
   My spirit starts to break.
I, once the wanton within the wall,
At their feet now faltering fall,
   And lure of love forsake.
Where I was precious, I now appal;
My manly mettle now is small,
   And those who, pleased, bespake
Me clothes and keep, life's wherewithal,
Now shrink as if I gave them gall.
   This, age and evil make.

Age and evil and other woe
   Follow me so fast
I think my heart will break in two.
Sweet God above, why should it so?
   How can this longer last?

My life was full of falsity:
My gleeman's name was Gluttony;
   He dwelt with me awhile.
For playfellow, came Pride with me;
My laundress's name was Lechery;
   Their friends were Fraud and Guile.
Covetousness carried my key;
Envy and Anger companioned me,
   Villains ugly and vile.
Lying prompted my every plea;
Both Sleep and Sloth, bedded with me,
   Waited on me awhile.

At whiles I dwell on thoughts of bliss,
   If bliss should ever be.
I then lament my ways remiss.
Lord who gave me life, grant this:
   That I from ill be free!

Such the life which long I bore.
Mercy, Lord, I'll sin no more,
   But bow to gain your grace.
Certainly they dog me sore,
Deceit and lies and such foul lore,
   Unseemly sins and base.

The word of God I would ignore,
And ever labour against his law:
   Now must I mend apace.
So pierced am I by sorrows sore
That I shall waste away before
   Bliss I again embrace.

Embracing bliss was all I sought
   When held in honour by all.
Like others, I hankered for high report,
Haughty as henchmen at the court,
   Or huntsman-chief in hall.

Dreadful Death is lurking there
To clasp this body cold and bare
   And take it torment-bound.
Comfortless and cast in care,
Like fading flower to death I fare;
   I feel my fatal wound.
No pleasures can my woes repair:
Before, Lord, grizzled grows my hair,
   Halt my earthly round!
I yearned with cravings many a year;
Which saddens my life with sick despair
   And treads it to the ground.

To ground by sin my soul is hurled.
   What remedy is meet,
But praise Our Lord who made the world,
And by his deed redeemed the world,
   And fall before his feet?

Ready I stand for death to smite:
   Done is my every deed.
May God above so grant us light
That of the saints we may have sight,
   And heaven as our meed!

74

The tears of weeping wet my cheek:
My wicked deeds and lack of wit
Plague my soul until I seek,
As Bible bids, atonement fit

For taking ladies' love in vain,
Which softly gleams with lovely light.
My songs have slandered it: their stain
Has robbed me of my lover's right.
  It sticks but is not fitting
  When it is said in song;
  Of women I have written
  Detractions vile and wrong.

I wrote that wrong because of Eve:
She had no need to hold the reins,
But caused mankind to groan and grieve,
And robbed us of our richest gains.
The One who stopped her cruel strife
Is hidden in the heart divine.
In her alit the Lord of Life,
Within her fairest flesh to shine.
  As sun that gleams through glass,[1]
  He shone within her form;
  No wicked woman was
  Since Jesus Christ was born.

What man could be so base and vile
As make such fair ones' tears to fall?
They live devoid of vice and guile,
And courteously, as hawks in hall.
My wicked words I thus repent:
That fickle flesh and blood's deceit
Defiled those fair ones, I lament
And contrite fall before their feet;
  Yes, at their feet fall low
  For falsehoods fifty-fold
  And calumnies, I know,
  Which traitor-like I told.

Though evil tales are told in town,
I shall scorn them in despite,
Since beauties blest with brows of brown
Bring only bliss and great delight.
Even a bitter heart would bring

---

1. A beautiful idea, often found in medieval devotional writing.

Peace from talk with one of them,
And priest and emperor and king
Should scorn to wait on none of them.
　To wait on woman's needs
　And serve with might and main
　Is best, for woman's deeds
　Redeemed the world from pain.

Now worldly woes have gone away
And joy has come, as all desire;
A mild Maiden's mighty way
Has freed us from affliction dire.
Such women I shall praise for ever
And in the house their aims fulfil.
At need I shall affirm I never
Wrote a word against their will.
　Such words I would not write,
　For now there is no need.
　This truth I now recite,
　As Richard first decreed.

Richard, root of reason right,
In poetry and rune and rhyme,
Of gentle maidens you can write
The finest verses of our time!
As gentle-tempered as a knight,
A scholar versed in mysteries,
In every house his fame is bright,
And nobles wish all joy were his.
　Good fortune now be his,
　And courtesy in hall!
　May he receive all bliss
　From ladies one and all!

75

O God, who does all deeds of might
　In heaven and here on earth below!
I went to waste by day and night,
　Both late and early was your foe,
And wrongly wrenched away from right,
　Although the laws were plain to know.
To you so full of grace and light
　All unprepared am I to go.

Little goodness have I got
    To go to him who bought us all!
Of what I did, and what I thought,
    The best is bitterer than the gall.
I knew the right, but liked it not;
    In folly I preferred to fall:
And when I look upon my lot,
    I know I am the worst of all.

O God who died upon the Rood,
    This world's perfection to fulfil,
For us you sweetly spilled your blood!
    But my deeds hit my heart with chill;
Against you stubbornly I stood,
    Early or late, hectic or still:
In all I did I find no good.
    Lord, upon me do your will!

In spirit I would never bow,
    Nor to my good Lord humbly go.
I made my love my hate, I vow,
    And dread of Christ I would not show.
No Jew is viler, I allow,
    And this I would the world should know.
Lord, have pity on me now,
    And lift me up, thus fallen low!

O God, whom all on earth shall heed,
    This world you have in kindly hold:
You came to earth to meet our need,
    For sinful us were bought and sold.
When death and judgement are decreed,
    And fates on day of doom are told,
Then shall we see your sweet wounds bleed,
    And our requests will not be bold.

Not bold am I to beg my plea,
    So vile and rash the life I led.
I did not walk by your decree;
    To wicked ways I turned my tread.
Rotten the root and branch of me!
    Your words and ways were wrong, I said.
Jesu, be my remedy!
    To make my peace I bow my head.

Ah Christ my Lord, what can I say?
　　My peace and quiet are broken quite;
At every thought I feel dismay,
　　For nothing that I did was right.
Unworthy I am to walk your way;
　　I serve you neither day nor night:
Yet grant your mercy: thus I pray,
　　O God, who does all deeds of might.

76[1]

Winter rouses all my grief:
Branches strip till they are bare,
And sighing in sorrow, I despair
　　That earthly pleasures come to nothing.

Fleeting joys, now here, now gone!
True it is, as many say,
Except God's will, all fades away.
　　Willy-nilly, we all shall die.

Seed I planted green now withers.
Jesus, your high purpose show:
Stave off hell, for when I go
　　From here, and where, I do not know.

77

Now fade the rose and lily-flower
That once, in summer's balmy hour,
　　Gave sweetly out their scent.
All queens of plenitude and power,
All ladies bright in palace bower,
　　By gliding death are pent.
If man will cast out fleshly lust,
　　On heavenly bliss being bent,
Then think of Jesus Christ he must,
　　Whose side by spear was rent.

1. The original is in a five-lined stanza, rhyming aaabb, which has a long, irregular last line.

On pleasure forth adventuring
From Peterborough at morning-spring,
  My secret love I weighed,
And grieving it and murmuring
To her who bore the heavenly King,
  For clemency I prayed:
'Beg your Son to grant us grace,
  (For us he dearly paid)
And save us from the loathsome place,
  That house for devils made!'

My heart was shuddering with dread
For fleshly sins on which I fed
  Of which my life was made.
I know not where I shall be led,
To joy or woe, when on the bed
  In death I shall be laid.
My hope in one sole Lady is,
  A Mother and a Maid;
For we shall come to heavenly bliss
  With her healing aid.

Better is her medicine
Than any mead or any wine;
  Her herbs are sweet of scent.
And sure, from Caithness to Dublin,
No doctor is so skilled and fine
  At curing discontent.
A man of vices manifold
  Who longs to change his bent
Can, without paying wealth or gold,
  Win health and high content.

Her cures of penance smoothly run:
My service to her shall be done
  As long as I have life:
To joy and freedom slaves have come
Through that noble, slender one:
  Praise to her blisses five!
Whenever man in sickness is,
  To reach her he should strive;
And through her grace are brought to bliss
  Maid and married wife.

May he who died upon the tree
Grant us sinners clemency,
   Prince of heavenly bowers!
Women, in your gaiety
Think of God's benignity,
   Which falls on us in showers.
Though bright and fair of face you be,
   Decay shall fade your flowers.
Jesu, honoured in high degree,
   Yet may your grace be ours!

78

Jesu, through your noble might,
   Grant to us your grace,
That so we may by day and night
   Contemplate your face.
In my heart it does me good
When I think of Jesu's blood
   Streaming down his side
From wounded heart to wounded foot:
For us he shed his own heart-blood
   From cruel wounds and wide.

When I think of Jesus dead,
   My heart is overthrown;
My soul turns wan and pale as lead
   For evils I must own.
That man must sink in woe and dread
Who does not muse on Jesus dead,
   His pain and suffering sore.
I weep for sins my evil bred,
And all of them I hope to shed,
   Both now and evermore.

Man on earth for bliss and joy,
   Who lies in shame and folly,
Were foolish did he not destroy
   And leave that sinning wholly.
All this world shall go away,
And then shall come the Judgement Day,
   When man goes underground.
May Jesus Christ who died in woe
Lead our souls to heaven that so
   In bliss we may be found!

Ponder, though you wanton be,
  The wounds God underwent,
Enduring cruel pain that we
  By death should not be rent.
For man he suffered and he died:
If man will take his word as guide
  And leave all infamy,
Then we shall come to happiness
And blisses more than we can guess
  In Jesu's company.

Gentle Jesus, mild and free,
  Upon the Cross there nailed,
Pierced with spear most cruelly,
  With scourges whipped and flailed;
All for man he suffered shame,
Though void of guilt and void of blame
  That day and every other.
Man, he loved you mightily
When he strove to make you free,
  And would become your brother!

79

With sadness in my song
  And grief at what I see,
I sigh and mourn the wrong
  Upon the gallows-tree,
Where Jesu fair and good
Lets fall his heart's blood
  For the love of me.
His moistening wounds let go
Their sweet unceasing flow:
  Mary, mournful be!

Upon a lofty down,
  For all to see who may,
A mile outside the town,
  At mid-hour of the day,
They raise on high the Cross.
His friends so dread his loss
  They shrink and blanch like clay.
The Cross stands fast in stone,
But Mary stands alone
  And says, 'Alas the day!'

When I see you there –
   Your two eyes bright with grace,
Your body cold and bare,
   Your pale and livid face –
Hung on the Cross on high
In streams of blood to die
   Between two robbers base,
Who more than I is grieved?
Mary, who weeps bereaved
   And sighs at the piteous place.

The nails are much too strong,
   The blacksmiths are too sly;
You bleed too long, too long,
   The Cross is raised too high,
The stones are wet with blood.
Ah, Jesu sweet and good,
   No friend of yours is by
Except Saint John in mourning,
And Mary sadly burning
   With grief that you should die.

When continually
   I sigh and make my moan,
Most hateful though it be,
   Yet wonder is it none;
When I see high uphung,
With bitter torment stung,
   Jesu, my loved one;
His wounds which grimly smart,
The spear which cleaves his heart,
   Thrust through flesh and bone.

Often when I wake,
   Shot through with grief and gall,
I sigh, my spirits ache,
   My thoughts are sorrow all.
Ah, man is mad to curse
By the Cross, for, worse,
   He sells for profit small
The Redeemer of our sin.
To bliss may he bring us in,
   Who dearly bought us all!

80

'Mother, stand firm beneath the Rood!
Look on your Son in cheerful mood;
Joyful, Mother, should you be.'
  'Son, how should I joyful stand?
I see your foot, I see your hand
Nailed upon the cruel tree.'

  'Mother, leave your tears behind!
I suffer death for all mankind;
No mortal sin I suffer for.'
  'Son, your hour of death I see;
The sword is at the heart of me,
As Simeon prophesied before.'

  'Mother, mercy! Let me die,
That Adam and his kin who lie
Forlorn I may redeem from hell.'
  'Son, my grief is death to know,
So grant I die before you go.
What words from me could sound so well?'

  'Mother, pity your children all,
And stem your bloody tears that fall:
They hurt me more than that I die.'
  'Son, I see your heart-stream flow
In blood to where I stand below:
Then how can eyes of mine be dry?'

  'Mother, I shall tell you why:
Better that I alone should die
Than all mankind to hell should go.'
  'Son, I see your body lashed,
Your feet and hands with deep wounds gashed:
No wonder that I suffer woe!'

  'Mother, listen to me well:
If I die not, you go to hell;
I undergo this death for you.'
  'Son, of my grieving think no ill,
Nor blame me that I sorrow still,
Your nature is so meek and true.'

'Mother, now you learn in care
What grief they have who children bear,
What grief it is with child to go.'
　'Son, such grief I know full well:
Unless it be the pain of hell,
I cannot think of greater woe.'

　'Mother, grieve your mother's woe,
For now a mother's lot you know,
Though virgin you of spotless life.'
　'Son, give help in word and deed
To all who cry to me their need –
The foolish woman, maid or wife.'

　'Mother, on earth I may not dwell:
My time is come to go to hell;
The third day I shall rise again.'
　'Son, beside you I shall go:
I die for all your wounds and woe
And death unequalled for its pain.'

When he rose, then died her sorrow:
Her bliss began the third morrow:
Joyful, Mother, were you then!
Lady, for that bliss begun,
Shield us from the Evil One,
And beg your Son to pardon sin!

Blessed are you, full of bliss.
Heaven may we never miss,
Through your Son's most tender might!
For that blood and cruel loss
You shed and suffered on the Cross,
Bring us, Lord, to heaven's light!

81

When I see blossoms thronging
　And hear the birds at song,
Then with sweet love-longing
　My heart is pierced and stung
All for a love that's new
And yet so sweet and true,
　It gladdens all my song.
And I know certainly
My joy and ecstasy
　To him alone belong.

When alone I stand
  And, looking on him, see
Him pierced through foot and hand
  With mighty nails three,
His gory head, and men
Still faithless to him when
  He suffers gloriously,
Greatly ought my heart
For love of him to smart,
  And sad and grieving be.

Jesu calm and meek,
  Give me strength and might
Most longingly to seek
  And love you as is right,
And torment undertake,
Sweet Mary, for your sake!
  Noble you are, and bright,
Maiden and Mother mild!
For love of him, your Child,
  Send us heaven's light.

Alas I know not how
  To turn with heart and brain
To him with lover's vow;
  For he with long harsh pain
And gashes deep and sore
Our ransom dearly bore.
  Such love none can explain.
His blood that to the ground
Fell from his sweet wound
  Redeemed us all from pain.

Jesu mild and sweet,
  I sing my song to you;
I hail you and entreat
  You always, as is due.
May all my sinning cease,
And may my penance release
  All earthly wrong I knew.
Sweet Jesu, when we go
From living here below,
  Then hold us close to you!

82

The heart of Man can hardly know
    How love of us has bound
The One who on the Cross let flow
    Redemption from his wound.
His love has saved us, made us whole and sound,
And hurled the grisly Devil underground.
Continually by night and day, he keeps us in his thought;
He will not lose what he so dearly bought.

He bought us with his holy blood;
    How could he grant us more?
He is so meek and mild and good,
    And free of sin therefore.
I say we should repent for evermore
And cry to Jesus, 'Mercy, we implore!'
Continually by night and day, he keeps us in his thought;
He will not lose what he so dearly bought.

He saw his Father greatly wroth
    At Man's most sinful fall:
With grieving heart he swore his oath
    That we should suffer all.
But then his sweet Son made his pleading call,
And begged that he might die and save us all.
Continually by night and day, he keeps us in his thought;
He will not lose what he so dearly bought.

He took from us the pains of death –
    Benign and gracious deed!
Sweet Jesus Christ of Nazareth,
    For heaven's reward we plead!
Of him on Cross why do we take no heed?
His freshly gaping wounds so grimly bleed.
Continually by night and day, he keeps us in his thought;
He will not lose what he so dearly bought.

His open wounds are bleeding fast;
    We must remember him:
Through him our pains of hell are past;
    He saved us all from sin.
For love of us his cheeks are growing thin:
He gave his blood for all his earthly kin.
Continually by night and day, he keeps us in his thought;
He will not lose what he so dearly bought.

Secular Poems   83

The heart of Man can hardly know
        What secret love can do,
Unless a lovely woman show,
        Who knows it through and through.
    The love of such is brief, and wayward too:
She took my lover's promise once, but calls me now untrue.
Continually for love of her I grieve in heavy thought;
    I think of her, but mostly see her not.

Today I'd call her by her name
        If I dared begin.
Among the folk of courtly fame
        She's fairest of her kin.
    Unless she loves me she'll commit a sin:
Alas for the man who loves a girl whom he can never win!
Continually for love of her I grieve in heavy thought;
    I think of her, but mostly see her not.

Crying, I fall before her face
        With, 'Lady, I implore
You grant your faithful lover grace!
        Be true to lovers' lore!
    Until you are, my heart with grief is sore,
For love's affliction pains me so that I can live no more!'
Continually for love of her I grieve in heavy thought;
    I think of her, but mostly see her not.

What bliss in that adored one's tower,
        With knight and servant throng!
And such the pleasures of her bower,
        With sport and courtly song.
    My woe, unless she loves me, will be strong:
Alas for the man whose lover is untrue and does him wrong!
Continually for love of her I grieve in heavy thought;
    I think of her, but mostly see her not.

Prettiest girl who breathes the air,
        My love, I welcome you
As many many times, I swear,
        As there are drops of dew,
    Or heavenly stars, or herbs of sweet or rue!
Content shall rarely come to men whose lovers are untrue;
Continually for love of her I grieve in heavy thought;
    I think of her, but mostly see her not.

84[1]

Spring's about with love again,
With blossom and with birds' refrain
   The top of pleasure bringing.
Daisies whitening all the dales,
The lovely notes of nightingales –
   Every bird is singing.
The song-thrush endlessly trills on,
For winter's misery is gone
   When the woodruff's springing.
A host of birds profusely sing
The joy and blessing of the spring,
   And set the woodlands ringing.

The rose puts on her reddening hue,
The leaves with ardour sprout anew,
   In the bright woods glowing.
The moon sends down her radiant light,
While lilies, lovely to the sight,
   Fennel and thyme are blowing.
Wild and wanton drakes abound;
Their mating calls to lovers sound
   Like stream serenely flowing.
The passionate man and others sigh,
And of that company am I,
   Distraught with love and wooing.

The moonbeams shed their lovely light,
And when the glorious sun shines bright,
   The sounds of bird-song swell.
The moistening dew on uplands falls,
Creatures utter secret calls,
   Their loving tales to tell.
Worms beneath the ground make love;
Women flaunt their pride above –
   The spring becomes them well.
If none of them can burn for me,
Then, lost to fortune, I shall flee
   And in the wild wood dwell.

1. The original has alliteration in every line.

85[1]

Between March and April,
　　When sprays begin to spring,
The little bird in bird-song
　　Delights and longs to sing.
　　And lost in love, I cling
　　To the fairest, sweetest thing.
　　Blisses may she bring
　　　　To me, her bonded one!

　　　　　　Grace and glorious luck are mine,
　　　　　　And sure, their sending is divine;
　　　　　　My love has left all womankind,
　　　　　　　　And lights on Alison.

Bright hair and body slender,
　　Tawny eyebrows sweet;
Her eyes of black show tender
　　When my own they meet.
　　Unless she takes me straight
　　To be her own true mate,
　　I shall be felled by Fate,
　　　　My earthly life fordone.

　　　　　　Grace and glorious luck, etc.

At night-time, tossing, waking,
　　(My cheeks turn pale for you)
For your sake, lady, aching,
　　I feel desire anew.
　　No wizard's words will do
　　To give her praises due:
　　Ah, neck of swan-like hue,
　　　　Fairest beneath the sun!

　　　　　　Grace and glorious luck, etc.

I weary like milling water,
　　With sleepless longing sore,
And lest my love be stolen,
　　I languish in her lure.
　　But better a while to endure
　　Than mourn for evermore.
　　Sweetest whom I adore,
　　　　Hear my orison!

1. Lines 1 and 3 of stanzas 1 and 4 of the translation are deficient in rhyme.

Grace and glorious luck are mine,
And sure, their sending is divine;
My love has left all womankind,
And lights on Alison.

86

Through Ribblesdale I'd like to ride,
And find the girls of fleshly pride,
    And have the one I would.
The fairest girl of blood and bone,
I'll seek her out where she is known,
    Among the great and good.
Her look, a beam of brilliant sun,
Gleams, or so the rumours run,
    On all the neighbourhood.
A lily, lovely, lissom, slender,
Her white shot through with roses' splendour,
    And sparkling gold her snood.

I see her head, a gleaming ray
That hits the sense at height of day,
    Or so it strikes my sight.
Her eyes are large and grey, and she,
When darting lovely looks at me,
    Arches her brows with light.
The moon that stands in heaven's height
Sheds not such radiance at night,
    For all its power and might,
As does her forehead in the day.
For her I mourn my life away
    And pall in deathly plight.

Nobly arched her brows appear,
With white between and not too near;
    Blissful life she knows.
For loving I am doomed to die.
Her speech, like spice, perfumes the sky,
    And seemly is her nose.
So long and lovely is her hair
That when it's falling free and fair
    My joy to rapture grows.
A lovely chin, a cheek which glows
With purest white and pink, and shows
    The red of flowering rose.

A pleasing mouth to frame her thought,
Lips red and true, expressly wrought
   A fine romance to read.
As sweetly set as any known,
Her teeth are white as whale-bone;
   Let courtly men take heed.
Her swan-like neck is truly set,
And longer than I ever met,
   A perfect pleasure indeed!
I'd rather wait for her to come
Than be the Pope and ride in Rome
   In pomp upon a steed.

When I behold her lily-white hand,
The palest parchment in the land
   It best appears to be.
Her look is sweet and mild as balm,
And long and glimmering each arm,
   As white as ivory.
Her fingers, made for holding fast;
If I could clasp her at the last,
   The world were bliss to me.
Her breasts like fruit of Eden both
Waver under linen cloth,
   As you yourself may see.

In beaten gold and brightly chased,
Her girdle grips her slender waist;
   Its tassel tips her toe.
Besides the emeralds, on it shine
Rubies carved by craftwork fine,
   And ranged in row on row.
The buckle is of whalebone,
And set in it there stands a stone
   That wards off every woe.
The water in which this stone is wet
Is changed to wine, and ever yet
   Who saw it, vouched it so.

A slender waist, a body and breast
In beauty ranking with the best,
   A phoenix without a peer!
Her woman's flanks are soft as silk
And whiter than the morning milk;
   Her looks are crystal clear.

And all the parts I have not named,
Unless a wonder were, are framed
    As well as might appear.
A man were blest in Jesu's sight
If he could lie with her at night,
    For he'd have heaven here.

87

A beauty white as whale's bone;
A golden bead, shining alone;
A turtle my heart is fixed upon,
    Earth's truest thing!
Her gaiety will not be gone
    While I can sing.

When blisses on this beauty pour,
Of all this world I ask no more
Than be alone with her and draw
    No word of strife.
I blame a lovely woman for
    My woes in life.

No beauty could be better wrought.
When to bed she's blithely brought,
Happy for him who knows her thought,
    That creature fair!
But well I know she loves me not,
    To my despair.

How shall a singer sweetly sing,
Afflicted so with suffering?
Dreadful death to me she'll bring
    Before my day.
Bow low to her, that lovely thing
    With eyes of grey!

Those eyes have dealt me agonies;
Her curving brows have brought me bliss:
Her comely mouth a man might kiss
    And be in heaven.
I'd gladly change my lot for his
    To whom she's given.

And if his mind were fair and free,
And worthy women I could see,
For her I'd give him any three,
    Without ado.
From hell to heaven, from sun to sea,
There's no one so discreet as she,
Nor half as generous: hark to me,
    You lovers true!

Yes, listen while my tale I tell.
I burn, distracted in a spell:
There is no hotter flame in hell
    Than lover's fire
When secret lover dare not tell
    His strong desire.

I wish her well, she wills me woe;
I am her friend, but she's my foe:
I think my heart will break in two
    With sighs and care.
With God's own greeting may she go,
    So white, so fair!

I wish I were a throstle-cock,
A bunting or a laverock,
    Sweet birds of the air!
Between her kirtle and her smock
    I'd hide, I swear.

88

I know of a beauty, a beryl most bright,
As lovely to look on as silver-foiled sapphire,
As gentle as jasper a-gleam in the light,
As true as the ruby, or garnet in gold.
Like onyx she is, esteemed in the height;
A diamond of worth when she's dressed for the day;
Like coral her lustre, like Caesar or knight;
Like emerald at morning, this maiden has might.
    My precious red stone, with the power of a pearl,
    I picked for her prettiness, excellent girl!

Her maiden-bloom's red, like the rose on the spray,
And lily-white loveliness shines in her face;
Like smallage, anise, alexanders' array,
Surpassing the spring-flower and periwinkle too,
Most glorious of girls in her fur-trimmings grey,
She blooms in her beauty like blue columbine,
The fairest of finely-robed women, I say,
As fragrant as sage or the small celandine.
    The sight of her beauty brings bliss: oh behold
    The salving, all-saving, long-sought marigold!

A parrot whose prattle's medicinal to stings
(I tell my sad tales to true turtle in tower);
A thrush of high fame that in fair palace sings;
A woodpecker, hawk, or a laverock untamed;
Merriest of maidens in all revellings,
But a forest-bred falcon, discreet in the vale,
And the wisest from Wirral to Wye in all things.
Her name's in a note of the nightingale:
    In Annot's her name: is it mentioned by none?
    Who rightly can guess it, then whisper to John.

A nutmeg, a mandrake with power from the moon;
A true cure as told of by tongues in high heaven;
Such liquorice will heal from the Lyn to the Lune;[1]
Such quick-salving sugar all searchers must seek.
Christ blesses her gladly and grants me my boon
When our darkly-hid doings are done in the daylight.
As green in its seed makes the gromwell known,
And the tops tell of cubeb and cummin, so she,
    Like cinnamon chested or fennel far-famed,
    Valerian or ginger or clove, is acclaimed.

She's mercy's reward and a marvellous cure;
As ready as Ragna to counsel with reason;
A Tegeu for truth and a Garwen for allure;
Bolder than Bjorn who challenged the boar.
Like Wylcadoun, wise and, in exploit, sure;
Fairer than Floris; like Craddock at court
Who alone could carve, her fame is secure;
More gracious than Hilde, and grace she shows me,
    Grace quickly given, this courteous one,
    As, gentle as Jonas, she joys in her John.

1. The Lyn is in Devonshire and the Lune in Lancashire.

89

Love hurts me with its craving,
And madness sends me raving,
   A girl so tortures me.
I never tire of seeing
That most enchanting being;
   I groan and cry my plea:
   Have pity on my wrongs,
Lady who brought me pain,
And make me whole again!
   To you my life belongs.

Best of beauties fair,
I languish in despair;
   Loose the bonds which stay me!
Let all your coolness cease,
And send me words of peace
   At once, before you slay me.
   I am restless like the roe;
Though all men show me hate,
My love shall not abate
   In spite of every foe.

Lady, my desire
For you is all on fire
   To honour you when I may.
Pity me, befriend me,
For since to death you send me,
   I die before my day.
   Believe my song, for I
In perfect faith shall do
All I have sworn to you
   Until the day I die.

As lily-white she goes,
Complexioned like the rose,
   She robs me of my rest.
Of girls discreet and wise
She proudly bears the prize
   As loveliest and best.
   This lady lives in the west,
The fairest of noble kind;
And heaven a man would find
   At night-time as her guest!

90

In Maytime in the merry dawn
The leaves are bright on hill and lawn
    And beasts to joy inclined.
On branches gorgeous blossoms grow,
And wanton folk a-wooing go:
    I have it much in mind.
I cannot think of finer flowers
Than brilliant ladies in their bowers
    By yearning love confined.
Such wonderful girls are in the West:
The one I worship is the best
    From Ireland into Ind.

Woman would be the worthiest thing
Created by our heavenly King,
    Did lovers not forswear.
For man inclines to lustihood
And shameful love, although he should
    A wife as booty bear.
The men of trust are far too few,
But girls consent in spirit true,
    Despite the subtle snare.
And then the trickster has betrayed
With plighted troth the pretty maid;
    His oaths are her despair.

Women, beware when fair and free
The fainer speaks his flattery,
    And note his honour's hue!
In towns from Leicester right to Lound,
And far and wide such men are found,
    Pretenders most untrue.
The trickster twists the truth astray,
And sometimes has his wicked way
    At secret rendezvous.
Ah, ladies fair, beware your fate
When self-reproach appears too late,
    And love has fettered you!

Women have such winsome hue
That none of them could be untrue,
   Did men not first betray.
Ah, beauties nobly born and fair!
When men come wooing, first beware
   Of peril's worldly sway.
Too late when lady lies abed,
Forlorn without her maidenhead,
   For so she's bound to stay.
Ah, fair of face and linen-clad!
If she'd hear me, gay and glad
   We'd settle straight away.

91

In April, when, as all can hear, the nightingale is singing,
When with leaf and grass and blossom woods are green and springing,
Then love into my heart its spear so keen and sharp is flinging.
Night and day it drinks my blood: with woe my heart is stinging.

All this year I've been in love, and I can love no more:
My sighing for your grace was endless, lover I adore,
But love is yet no nearer me, and that afflicts me sore.
Sweet darling, I have loved you long, so hear me, I implore.

Sweet darling, let me beg of you a single loving speech,
For while I live, no other girl would I in love beseech.
With love of yours, beloved sweet, more blisses I might reach;
A loving kiss from your dear mouth would be my curing leech.

Sweet darling, let me beg of you a single loving favour:
If you love me, as men say, and I but dimly savour,
And if you wish it, give your love a far more open flavour,
For I am so obsessed with you, my sickened spirits quaver.

From Lincoln, Lindsey, Lound, Northampton, round for many a mile,
I've never seen a prettier girl who could my heart beguile.
Sweet darling, let me beg you, be my lover for a while.
     My woe in song I must lament
     To her who caused my discontent.

92

Riding in a wood unknown,
　　I chanced upon a pretty prize;
Like glistening gold she gleamed and shone,
　　And never was girl in gayer guise.
I asked her, if it were her will,
　　To tell her father's name, but she
Told me to leave her, took it ill,
　　And said she shunned discourtesy.

HE: 'Most courteous one, now hear my plea!
　　I speak no spite, I pose no care:
From trials and troubles I'll make you free,
　　And give you richest robes to wear.'

SHE: 'Clothes to wear well worth the name
　　I own, and take my pleasure in:
Yet better ill-clad, not bearing blame,
　　Than richly robed and sunk in sin.
Your way being won, the vagabond
　　You'll play and pleasure will be slight.
Better for me to make firm bond
　　Than fall, and grieve my fallen plight.'

HE: 'Misgivings vex your mind no more!
　　To you, I swear, all honour's due.
I'll hold until my hair is hoar
　　To every oath I've sworn to you.
Why loath to trust me longer than
　　This lighting of my love on you?
Another might press for such long span
　　You'd never dash him with 'Adieu!''

SHE: 'Such counsel I might quickly rue
　　When all my peace of mind were gone,
For soon you'd seek a lover new,
　　My nine days' wonder being done.
Then see me starve, a homeless thing,
　　Scorned and spurned at every door,
Estranged from kin and told to cling
　　To him I had embraced before.

'But better to marry a man of style,
  Who'd kiss and clip me courteously,
Then basely wed a blackguard vile,
  Who'd kill me sooner than set me free.
The best for both of us, I know,
  Is, you take me and I take you,
For though I swore I'd answer 'No',
  God's doing no one may undo.

'I do not fear to break my oath,
  Not being a witch or wizard fey.
I am a maid, a state I loathe,
  And want a lover who won't betray.'

93

HE: 'My death I love, my life I hate, all for a lady fair;
    That she is bright as morning light, too well I am aware:
    Like summer leaf whose greenness goes, I wither in despair.
    To whom then, thought availing not, shall I make known my
        care?

'Sighing, grief and deadly sorrow hold my heart so fast,
I fear I shall become distracted if it longer last.
With just a word from you, my love, my care and grief were past.
What gain to you to blight my life and make it stand aghast?'

SHE: 'Scholar, be quiet! You are a fool. No more I wish to chide you.
     You'll never see that day alive when I shall lie beside you.
     If you are taken in my bower, scandal shall deride you.
     Better to plod on foot than on an evil horse to ride you.'

HE: 'Alas, why say you so? I am your man, so pity me,
    For you are always in my thoughts, wherever I may be.
    The scandal would be yours if love for you were death of me;
    So let me live and be your love, and you my lover be.'

SHE: 'Be quiet, fool, I named you rightly; can't you stop that din?
     By day and night in wait for you lie Father and all his kin.
     If in my bower you're caught they will not stop, from fear of sin,
     Imprisoning me and killing you, and then your death you'll win!'

HE: 'Sweetest lady, change your mind; you fill me with distresses,
    And now I am as full of woes as once I was of blisses:
    Yet at your window fifty times we clung exchanging kisses,
    Whose pledge has power to make a lover hide his spirit's stresses.'

SHE: 'Alas, why say you so? You thus my pain of love renew.
A scholar was my lover once; his love to me was true;
The day he had no sight of me, he never gladness knew.
I loved him better than my life; what good does lying do?'

HE: 'While I was a scholar at school, I learned all kinds of lore;
And now with pangs of love for you I suffer anguish sore,
An outlaw in the forest far from home and human door.
Sweet lady, show me pity now, for I can say no more.'

SHE: 'You seem indeed to be a scholar, you speak so soft and still:
For love of me you never shall endure such pain and ill.
Father, mother and all my kin shall never thwart my will;
So you be mine, and I'll be yours, and all your joy fulfil.'

Sir Orfeo

'Sir Orfeo', on the poet's admission, is a ' Breton lay'. The word 'lay' means, in English as in French, a song or lyric: it was only after the time of Marie de France, who professed to derive her poems from Breton sources (originality was not respectable in the Middle Ages: one was expected to have a reputable source for any creative work), that the term 'Breton lay' came to mean a short romantic narrative in verse, either for reading or for chanting to some kind of musical accompaniment. However, no lays in the Breton language have survived, if indeed there ever were any. All that can be said about the very few in English is that they seem to have a strongly Celtic atmosphere, even when their immediate sources are French. According to Sisam, ' "Sir Orfeo" appears to have been translated from a French source into south-western English at the beginning of the fourteenth century.' The lofty romantic spirit of the poem may be compared with that of Chaucer's Franklin's Tale, which the Franklin defines as a Breton lay. Although the Franklin's Tale came ultimately from ancient Sanskrit, and 'Sir Orfeo' from Ovid's version of the Greek myths, both stories, as we have them, are thoroughly medieval in spirit.

'Sir Orfeo' is a simple essay in one aspect of the philosophy of courtly love. Before the events recounted in the lay, its hero has been transformed and ennobled by the love of an ideal woman. Hence the unquestioning rightness of his every thought and action: not for him the occasional defeat with ignominy, the errors of judgement, the doubts, backslidings into sin, of the chevalier in quest of his lady. Conquest and experience of female perfection have made him a paragon, so that when the underground marauders irrupt into his castle paradise with their chaos, the ceremonial epiphany of knightly virtue, in the mere performance of duty, brings grace and reward to the hero, and restores harmonious order to the society of which he is chief.

In the Greek original, the fallible Orpheus looked back and lost his lady. The contrasting success of the medieval Orfeo is not to be thought of as having been engineered to provide a popular happy ending to a story containing the ingredients of tragedy – as if the principles of Nahum Tate's *King Lear* had been applied in a medieval re-working of Greek myth. From the first few words after the prologue, 'Sir Orfeo' proceeds as a charmingly solemn demonstration of the invincibility of chivalric love. Orfeo, though almost dead with grief at the rape of his lady, knows his proper course without needing to reflect, and does not even hesitate at the dread entrance of the underworld. Similarly, his steward, left to rule in the king's absence, does not for one second harbour thoughts of usurping power: his love is perfect service.

The poem falls into a category common in Celtic lore in having the Rash Promise as theme – another facet which it shares with the Franklin's Tale. The lady in Chaucer is excused the fulfilment of her promise only through the chivalry of her admirer, but Orfeo, by his courage in searching out his wife in the underworld, wins the right not to fulfil his promise, which is

> ... now that I have lost my Queen ...
> I'll never look on woman more.

The repeated tributes to the quality of Orfeo's harping, firstly in his own court, then to the creatures of the wilderness, then to the beings of the underworld, and at last in Winchester again, throw some light on the mystery of medieval music. It could uplift, it could cure. And the undercurrent of harping flowing through our minds from the beginning of the poem prepares us for the wonderful dance of the hunting ghosts, which provides the emotional basis for the ensuing recognition scene between Orfeo and Heurodis. In this, after the falcons have sighted their prey, Orfeo matches them by spying out his wife. Music consoles the steward and reminds him of his lost lord, and music concludes the poem, with joyful weeping for the restoration of the marriage and the kingdom.

In this romance, for all that the poet, in true English style, is more concerned with telling his tale than in moralizing upon it, all is ceremony according to custom. When caught by the enchanters, Heurodis is occupied as all courtly ladies should be, playing beside an orchard in the love- and adventure-month of May. She and her husband, and the only other royal person mentioned, the King of Fairyland, always have retinues, which are often precisely numbered. Then, as in so many romances, a castle is described, in this case that of the Fairy King, which is as bright as the New Jerusalem in 'Pearl', and contrasts with the hideous wilderness of Orfeo's exile, where 'Vicious snakes writhe on the ground'.

This wilderness often appears in medieval literature. The hero of 'The Nut-Brown Maid' goes there because he is 'a banished man'; crazed lovers flee there (see poems nos. 84 and 93), knights like Sir Gawain have to travel through it on perilous quests, and there, too, can be found the 'wodwose', the wild man of the woods. Writers considered it a savage, twilit realm, where outcasts were at the mercy of ogres, monsters and demons, and no doubt many people thought of the actual waste lands of medieval England, which were extensive, in the same way. This wilderness is just one marvellous element in a lay whose whole subject is described, at the end, as 'this marvel'.

The original is written, like many verse romances, in rhymed couplets with lines of uneven, but generally octosyllabic, length. In this translation, preservation of the narrative flow has often been preferred to strict adherence to the rhyme scheme.

94
SIR ORFEO

We often read and find set down
What scholars tell us of the lays;
That those for harp have most renown
And tell of themes of highest praise.
Of weal or woe these lays may tell,
Of joy or jollity as well;
Some of treachery, some of guile,
In chance events that once befell;
Some are jests, some ribald tales,
And some there are of Fairyland.
But of all things that men may see,
Mostly of love in truth they be.
These lays belong to Brittany,
Were there composed and after written,
Of famous deeds of olden days:
Of these the Bretons made their lays.
If ever to their ears there came
Accounts of any deed of fame,
They spiritedly took their harps,

Made song of it, gave it a name.
   Of mighty deeds that once befell,
Not all of them, but some I know.
Listen, sirs, and I shall tell
And sing the lay 'Sir Orfeo'.

   Sir Orfeo was a king of might
In England and a noble lord,
Bold and valiant in the fight
A generous and a courteous knight.
His father came of Pluto's line,
His mother of Juno's, both divine
(Or so men called them for a time
For feats they did, much spoken of).
For Orfeo, above all things
The art of harping had his love:
And all good harpers were assured
Of honoured welcome from that lord.
He loved to play the harp himself,
And with devoted mind and grace
So studied that his harper's art
Was not surpassed in any place.
And never a man was born on earth
Who sat before Sir Orfeo,
Listening to the music's flow
But thought he was in Paradise,
Delighting in eternity,
His harping made such melody.
   This king held sway in Traciens,[1]
A city nobly fortified;
That Winchester then had the name
Of Traciens is not denied.
The king possessed a queen of fame,
The Lady Heurodis her name;
Of all the women of flesh and blood
Not one could be as fair and good,
And full of love: none could express
In words her perfect loveliness.
   It so befell in early May,
When warm and merry is the day,
And gone are all the winter's showers,
And every field is full of flowers,

1. From 'Thrace'!

And glorious blossoms gay and fair
Put forth on branches everywhere,
That this same Lady Heurodis
And two fair maids one morning-tide
Went out to play in happiness
At a pretty orchard-side;
To see the flowers spread and spring
And to hear the song-birds sing.

   There they sat them down all three
Beneath a lovely orchard-tree,
And straight away this comely queen
Fell asleep upon the green.
The maidens dared not break her sleep,
But let her lie in slumber deep,
And so she slept till afternoon,
When morning-tide was wholly gone.
As soon as she awoke, she cried,
And fearful clamour filled the place.
She wrung her hands and thrashed her feet,
And blood ran where she scratched her face.
Her sumptuous robe she tore in rents,
Deranged, distracted in her sense.
The maidens dared no longer stay
Beside the queen, but took their flight,
And at the palace straight away
They cried aloud to squire and knight
That Heurodis was mad or ill,
And told them they must hold her still.
Then out went knights, and ladies too,
Sixty maids in retinue,
And coming to the orchard found
The queen and raised her from the ground,
And brought her home to bed at last,
And there restrained her, held her fast.
But still she cried in great dismay,
And tried to rise and run away.

   When Orfeo heard, it grieved him more
Than any other thing before.
To the chamber with ten knights he went,
And there he looked upon his wife,
And spoke in pitiful lament:
'What ails you, my beloved life,
That you, ever so calm and still,

Now cry aloud in accents shrill?
Your body, white and excellent,
Is by your nails all torn and rent.
Alas! Your hue of rosy red
Is wan, as if my queen were dead;
And then besides, your fingers small
Are pale and bloody one and all.
Alas! Your loving eyes now show
As those of one who sees his foe.
Ah Lady! Mercy, pity me,
And cease these cries of misery.
What ails you and whence came it? How
Can cure be found to help you now?'

   And then all quiet she lay at last;
And as she wept, her tears fell fast,
And to the king she said these words:
'Alas! Sir Orfeo my lord,
Since we came together first
We never crossed each other in strife,
For I have loved you as my life
Always, just as you loved me.
But now our lives must separate be:
Fare you well, for I must go.'

   'Alas!' said he. 'You seal my doom:
Where will you go, and then to whom?
Wherever you go, there I shall go,
And where I go, there you shall go.'

   'No, no, sir, that cannot be so:
Now let me, leaving nothing out,
Tell you how it came about.
As I lay this morning-tide
Sleeping by our orchard side,
There came to me a troop of knights,
Fine to see and armed to rights,
Who told me to come hurrying
To audience with their lord the king.
To this I boldly answered no,
I neither dared nor wished to go.
So back they spurred with utmost speed,
And then their king came straight away
With a host on snow-white steeds,
At least a hundred knights, or more,
And damsels too, above five score.

Their lovely clothes were milky white,
And never yet there struck my sight
Beings so excellently bright.
A crown the king wore on his head,
Not silver, nor gold that glitters red,
But it was of a precious stone,
And brightly like the sun, it shone.
The moment that he came to me
He seized me irresistibly,
And force perforce he made me ride
Upon a palfrey at his side,
And took me to his citadel,
A palace equipped and furnished well,
And showed me castles there, and towers,
Rivers, forests, woods with flowers,
And all the wealth of his domain.
And then he brought me home again,
And in our orchard said to me:
"See, Lady, that tomorrow you be
Here beneath this orchard-tree,
For then you must come back with me
And live with us eternally.
If you resist in any degree,
You shall be fetched, wherever you are,
And limb from limb be torn apart,
Till you are past all help and cure.
Though torn apart, yet still be sure
You shall be fetched away by us."

When Orfeo heard this matter, thus
He cried: 'Alas! and woe, alas!
Better it were I lost my life
Than so to lose the queen my wife.'
He asked advice of every man,
But help King Orfeo, no man can.
The morrow morning being come,
Orfeo quickly grasped his arms
And took ten hundred knights with him,
Each stalwart stoutly armed and grim,
And with Queen Heurodis went he
Right to that same orchard-tree.
They made a wall of shields all round
And swore that they would hold that ground
And die to a man that very day

Before the queen were fetched away.
But all the same, from in their midst
The queen was spirited away
By magic; none could know or say
What became of her that day.

    Then they cried and wept their woes.
The king into his chamber goes,
And swoons upon the floor of stone,
Lamenting with such grief and moan
That in him life was almost spent;
But all this brought no betterment.

    He called his nobles to the hall,
Earls and barons, famous all,
And when they were assembled there,
'My lords,' he said, 'before you here,
My high steward I designate
To rule my kingdom from this date:
In my place he shall remain
To govern my entire domain.
For now that I have lost my queen,
The fairest lady ever seen,
I'll never look on woman more,
But to the wilderness I'll go,
And with the wild beasts evermore
I'll dwell in forests stark and hoar.
And when you hear my life is spent,
Summon together a parliament,
And then elect yourselves a king,
And do your best in everything.'

    Then there was weeping in the hall
And mighty outcry from them all;
Scarcely could the old or young
For grief give utterance with tongue.
Then down upon their knees they fell
And begged him, if it were his will,
To stay with them, and not to go.
'Have done!' said he. 'It shall be so.'

    He left his kingdom and was gone,
With only a pilgrim's mantle on.
All other clothing he forsook;
No kirtle, hood, or shirt he took.
But yet he had his harp, and straight
Barefoot left the city gate.

With him then no man might go.
  Alas! What tears there were and woe,
When he that had been king with crown
Went so poorly out of town!
Through wood, and over heath and down,
Into the wilderness he went.
Nothing he found to bring content,
But ever lived in languishment.
Once, grey and varied furs he wore,
Had purple linen on his bed:
Now he lies on the rugged moor
With leaves and grass upon him spread.
He, once the lord of castles, towers,
Rivers, forests, woods with flowers,
Now, when come the snow and frost,
Must make his royal bed of moss.
He who had most noble knights
And ladies before him kneeling down,
Only looks on loathsome sights:
Vicious snakes writhe on the ground.
He who lived a life of plenty,
With meat and drink, and every dainty,
Must dig the earth and work all day
Before he find his fill of roots.
In summer he lives on wild fruits
And berries, little good to him.
In winter nothing can he find
But grasses, roots, bark, and rind.
These rigours were so cruel and hard,
His body was all thin and scarred.
Lord! Who could paint the suffering
Through ten long years of this poor king?
All black and shaggy his beard had grown,
And to his girdle-place hung down.
His harp, in which lay all his glee,
He hid within a hollow tree;
But when the sky was clear and bright,
He went and took it instantly
And harped on it for pure delight.
Throughout the woods the music thrilled,
And all the beasts of forest field
For very joy came round him there,
And all the birds that ever were

Came and sat on branches near
To hear his harping to the end,
The sound so sweetly filled the air:
But when his tuneful harping ceased,
Beside him stayed no bird or beast.

On burning mornings often there
He saw the King of Fairyland
Hunting round him with his band
With dim crying and blowing sounds
Amid the baying of the hounds.
They caught no prey, nor could he tell
What afterwards to them befell.
At other times before his eye
A mighty multitude went by,
Ten hundred well-accoutred knights
Each equipped and armed to rights,
Fierce of face and bold in manner,
Displaying many a splendid banner;
And each his naked sword was showing.
He never knew where they were going.
At other times came other sights;
Came dancing ladies, dancing knights,
Elegant in poise and dress,
With skilful steps and quiet grace;
To trumpet-sound and tabour-beat,
All manner of music, moved their feet.

And then he saw, one certain day,
Sixty ladies riding by
As blithe and fair as birds on spray,
With not a man in all their band.
Each bore a falcon on her hand
And hawking rode beside the river,
Which many game-birds made their haunt –
Mallard, heron, cormorant.
And when they from the water rise,
The falcons mark them with their eyes,
And each one strikes his victim dead.
Orfeo watched and laughing said:
'By my faith, most pleasant game!
I shall join them, in God's name!
Such things I knew in former days.'
He rises, thither makes his way,
But then a lady meets his gaze:

He clearly understands and sees
By every token, that she is
His queen, the Lady Heurodis.
He looks on her, and she on him
In longing, but no word is said.
Then when she saw the wretched state
Of him who had been rich and great,
The tears came falling from her eyes.
This the other ladies saw,
And forced the queen to ride away,
And she could stay with him no more.

   'Alas, my sadness now!' he said.
'Why will not death now strike me dead?
Alas! How miserable am I
To see this sight, and then not die!
Alas! Too long my wretched life
When I dare not bid my wife
To hasten to my side, or speak.
Alas! Why does my heart not break?
In faith,' said he, 'whatever betide,
Wheresoever these ladies ride,
That self-same way I'll follow them,
For life and death I do contemn.'
He girded up his mantle then,
And hung his harp upon his back,
And sternly followed on their track,
Staying for neither stone nor stock.
Then rode the ladies in at a rock,
And Orfeo followed, pausing not.
Three miles or more within the rock
He came upon a pleasant plain,
As bright as sun on summer's day,
Smooth and level and wholly green,
Where neither hill nor dale was seen.
And there upon the plain he saw
A castle of amazing height,
A royal one whose outer wall,
Like crystal, glittered clear and bright;
And on it stood a hundred towers,
Marvellous forts of mighty power.
Straight from the moat buttresses flew,
Rich gold arches of splendid hue.
The vaulting of the roofs was wrought

With carved creatures of every sort.
Within, the spacious presence-rooms
Were built throughout of precious stones.
The poorest column one might behold
Was wholly made of burnished gold.
So all that land had endless light,
For all the time of dark and night
The precious stones with lustre shone
As brightly as the noonday sun.
No man could tell or reach with thought
The sumptuousness that there was wrought.
By every sign one might surmise
It was the court of Paradise.

   Into this castle went the ladies:
Wishing to follow if he might,
King Orfeo knocked upon the gate.
The ready porter came out straight
And asked what business brought him there.
'I am a minstrel,' he declared.
'If it be to his accord,
I come to please this castle's lord
With music.' And the porter then
Unbarred the gate, and let him in.

   Once inside, he looked about
And saw, disposed within the court,
A host of people, thither brought
As being dead, though they were not.
Some, though headless, stood erect,
From some of them the arms were hacked,
And some were pierced from front to back,
And some lay bound and raging mad.
And some on horse in armour sat,
And some were choked while at their food,
And some were drowning in a flood,
And some were withered up by fire;
Wives lay there in labour-bed,
Some raving mad, and others dead.
And also many others lay
As if asleep at height of day;
Like that they had been snatched away
And taken there by fairy riders.
There he saw his own dear life,
The Lady Heurodis his wife,

Asleep beneath an orchard-tree.
He knew by her clothes that it was she.

And having seen these marvels all,
He went into the royal hall,
And there he saw a seemly sight:
Upon a dais serenely bright
There sat the king, the master there,
And the queen, most sweet and fair.
Their crowns, their clothing, shone so bright,
His eyes could hardly stand their light.

When he had looked on everything,
He kneeled down before the king
And said, 'If, lord, your will it be,
You shall hear my minstrelsy.'
The king replied, 'What man are you
To come here now? For neither I
Nor any of my retinue
Have ever asked or sent for you.
And since the time my reign began,
If ever I found a reckless man
Who dared to visit us, I then
Promptly sent for him again.'[1]
'My lord, believe me well,' said he,
'A poor minstrel is all you see;
And, sir, it is the way with us
To call at many a noble house,
And though unwelcome we may be,
Yet must we offer our minstrelsy.'

Then down he sat before the king,
And took his tuneful harp in hand,
And skilfully he set the strings,
And plucked from them such heavenly airs,
That everybody who was there
About the palace came to hear,
And lay before the harpist's feet,
They thought his melody so sweet.
The king, attentive, sitting still,
Listened with his utmost will.
The music brought enjoyment keen
To him and to his gracious queen.

Now when his harping reached its end,
Then to Orfeo said the king,

1. Grim irony common to supernatural dealers in death.

'Your playing, minstrel, I commend.
Now you may ask for anything,
And you shall have your whole request:
So speak, and put it to the test.'
Said he, 'Then give me of your grace
That lady there, of fairest face,
Who sleeps beneath the orchard-tree.'
'No,' said the king, 'that shall not be!
You'd make an ill-assorted pair,
For you are lank and beggarly,
And she is spotless, bright, and fair.
Therefore it would be villainy
To see her in your company.'
Said Orfeo, 'Most noble king,
Yet still more villainous a thing
To hear your mouth speak out a lie;
For since you did not specify
What I should ask, I must receive,
And to your promise you must cleave.'
Replied the king, 'Since that is so,
Then take her by the hand and go!
Have joy of her in everything.'

    Orfeo knelt and thanked the king.
He took fair Heurodis by the hand
And with her swiftly left that land
By the self-same road that he had come.

    Long ways they journeyed from the place
And came to Winchester, his home.
There no man recognized his face,
But fearing that he might be known,
He did not dare to make his way
Beyond the outskirts of the town,
But in a narrow billet lay,
Took lodgings with a beggar-man
Both for himself and for his wife,
As minstrel folk of lowly life.
He asked what tidings in the land,
What ruler held it in his hand,
And that poor beggar in his cot
Gave all the news and stinted not:
How their queen, ten years before,
Was snatched away by fairy power,
And how their king went off alone,

An exile in a land unknown:
And how the steward ruled as king;
And told him many another thing.

    The morrow, at mid-morning-tide,
He made his wife remain behind
And, borrowing the beggar's rags,
He slung his harp upon his back
And went into the city's ways,
Showing himself to people's gaze.
Earls and barons bold and grim,
Townsmen and ladies looked on him.
'Look! What fellow is that?' they said.
'How long his hair hangs from his head!
His beard reaches to his knee:
He is as withered as a tree!'
And as he walked about the street,
His own high steward he chanced to meet,
To whom he called with piercing cry,
'Have mercy on me, Steward! I
Am a harper of a heathen nation;
Help me in my desolation!'
The steward said, 'Come with me, come:
Of what I have, you shall have some.
I welcome all good harpers here
For Orfeo's sake, who held them dear.'

    The steward sat at the castle board,
And round him many a noble lord.
Trumpeters and tabourers,
Many harpers, fiddlers were
Making music one and all
While Orfeo, motionless in hall,
Listened. When they all were still,
He loudly tuned his harp with skill,
And played on it the sweetest air
That ever mortal heard with ear:
The sound delighted each man there.

    The steward looked with searching eyes:
At once the harp he recognized.
'Minstrel, by your life, I vow,'
Said he, 'that you shall tell me now
Where you got this harp, and how.'
'My lord,' said he, 'in lands unknown
Wandering a waste alone,

I found there in a dip remains
Of one who had been rent by lions,
And torn by teeth wolfish and sharp.
Beside him there I found this harp;
And that is quite ten years ago.'
'Oh,' said the steward. 'What utter woe!
That was my lord Sir Orfeo.
Ah wretched me, what shall I do,
My lord being lost, and I forlorn?
Alas, that ever I was born!
That such hard fate should be ordained,
And such vile death should be his end!'
Then down he fell and lay as dead.
The barons raised him up and said
Such was the course of destiny;
For death there is no remedy.

King Orfeo could tell by then
His steward was a faithful man
Who loved him as he ought to do;
So standing up for all to view,
He said, 'Sir Steward, hear this thing!
If I were Orfeo the king,
And had endured great suffering
In barren wastes for many a day,
And had won my queen away
From Fairyland, and safe and sound
Had brought her to the city bounds,
And lodged that queen of noble grace
In a lowly beggar's place,
And come to court in guile and stealth,
Unmarked by royalty or wealth,
To put your fealty to the proof,
And found, as now I do, such truth,
No reason would you have to repent:
And certainly, in any event,
You should be king, my day being spent.
But had you hailed my death, no doubt
At once you would have been cast out.'

Then all the company perceived
That he was Orfeo indeed.
The steward gazed at him and knew,
Leapt up and overthrew the board
And fell before his King and Lord.

So did every noble there,
And with one voice they all declared,
In gladness that his life was spared,
'You are our Lord, sir, and our King!'
They led him to a room with speed
And bathed him there and shaved his beard,
And robed him as a king indeed.
And afterwards they went and brought
The queen with lofty pomp to court,
With every kind of minstrelsy.
Lord! What mighty melody!
For very gladness wept they then
To see them come safe home again.
Now is Orfeo crowned anew,
And Heurodis, his own queen, too.
And when their long lives reached their end,
The steward was king, and ruled the land.

    Later, Breton harpers heard
How this marvel had occurred,
And made of it a pleasing lay,
And gave to it the name of the king.
So 'Orfeo' it is called today;
Fine is the lay, and sweet to sing.
    Thus did Orfeo quit his care:
    God grant that all of us so fare!

Two Comic Verse Tales

Like so many poems translated for this book, 'Dame Siriz and the Weeping Bitch' and 'The Fox and the Wolf in the Well' survive on a single manuscript, in this case one which is thought to have been written in Worcester Priory in about 1280. Without the wild humour of these poems, the poetic remains of thirteenth-century England would be both poorer and more limited in scope.

'Dame Siriz' is the first English fabliau. In France the many fabliaux provided the anti-masque for aristocratic poems about courtly love, knightly heroism, and saintly endurance: their lively satire scorned conventional morals and was usually anti-clerical. The story of a virtuous wife tricked, during her husband's absence, into surrendering her chastity to a crafty holy man is probably of oriental origin: it is found in many languages, and naturally takes the tone of its adoptive background. The English version is less concerned with the mechanism of courtly love than the French, and is especially good in the way that it maintains action and irony. In particular, the unintentional innuendo of Margery's opening speeches, and the condescending priestliness of Willikin's words throughout, are marks of a genuine comic writer. The tone of the poem is equivocal, in the sense that we are prepared either for the wooer to be rebuffed and humiliated, or for the ending we are given. Either way, the result would be funny, but the actual ending takes us joyously beyond the pale of respectability. And as for Margery, to judge by her earlier remarks when contemplating the 'faithless act', and her enthusiasm for whatever course she happens to be following, there appears to be little danger of Lucrece-like remorse ensuing.

McKnight notes that even such a bawdy and anti-clerical tale as this could attract the devout allegorizers. The chaste wife is the soul purified by baptism; the absent husband is Christ; the lover is worldly vanity; the go-between is the Devil; and the bitch is 'the hope of long life and too much presuming on the mercy of God because, just as that bitch was weeping from mustard, so hope frequently afflicts the soul'.

This version of the tale was presumably composed in East Anglia, where Boston (the town of Saint Botolph, patron of sailors) was the chief east-coast port after London, and a great market centre. McKnight notes many eastern forms of language mingled with the western of the scribe. 'Dame Siriz' is all in dialogue but for the brief narrative sections, which do not exceed forty lines altogether; and since the only fragment of medieval secular drama which has come down to us, 'De Clerico et Puella', concerns a girl's rejection of just such a wooer as Willikin, it has been thought fit, in the present translation, to allot the narrative to a minstrel, and so make the poem fully dramatic, for performance by four readers. The poet has not been precisely followed in his wayward alternation between couplets and tail-rhyme stanzas.

'The Fox and the Wolf in the Well' is the only medieval English beast-epic, and is one of the tales found in *Le Roman de Renard*. The story, like that of 'Dame Siriz', is found in many languages, but McKnight states that the buckets, which add so much to the humour, figure only in western versions. The dialect is southern English.

The tales about beasts, like the fables, are intended as satire and comment on human doings, and naturally carry their morals. The lessons of 'The Fox and the Wolf' are that one should not be a glutton; and that one should not be made foolish by love or trust false friends. But the poet also enriches his tale with gibes at cuckolded simpletons, and at friars who regard their morning devotions as a bore. The central joke, the confession and shrift of the wolf at the hands of the foxy friend who has cuckolded him, links the poem with 'Dame Siriz' in its hilarious anti-clericalism.

In both these comic poems, occasional liberties have been taken with the text, in an attempt to find an acceptable equivalent for medieval humour.

95
DAME SIRIZ AND THE WEEPING BITCH

MINSTREL: When I was once out walking,
I heard some fellows talking
    Of a man most proud and clerkish.
A swot he was, most pert,
And smooth beneath his shirt,
    And got up mighty sparkish.

This chap was nearly mad
With loving; which was bad,
    Because the girl was married.
For her he thumped his chest;
He couldn't sleep or rest –
    A load of love he carried.

The fellow lashed his mind
In pondering how to find
    A way to have the lady.
And as it chanced, one day
The husband went away
    On business straight or shady.

At once our hero made
His way to where she stayed –
    A fancy habitation!
There in the hall he found her
With natty finery round her
    And made this declaration:

WILLIKIN: Now may almighty God be here!

MARGERY: If I deserve a bit of cheer,
    You're welcome at my fire.
Come in! And if you want it so
Sit down, and kindly let me know
    What is your desire.

For by our Lord, the heavenly king,
If I can do a single thing
    That you may find diverting,
I shall oblige, as you will find,
And doing what you have in mind,
    Find nothing disconcerting.

WILLIKIN: May God requite you, lady, if
        You don't betray me in a tiff,
          Or hear me with displeasure.
        I'll tell you what I've come to do;
        But should my business anger you,
          My pain would pass all measure.

MARGERY: Oh, never fear, dear Willikin!
        I'd not commit the shameful sin
          Of thwarting all your yearning
        For any thing I might possess.
        I never studied churlishness,
          Nor shall I now start learning.

        You may utter all your will,
        And I shall listen sitting still
          To any good suggestion:
        And if it's right what you require,
        Then I shall do what you desire
          Without the slightest question.

        And though your words should bring me shame,
        I'd never saddle you with blame,
          So don't be apprehensive.

WILLIKIN: Now, lady, that I have your leave,
        If I were churl enough to grieve,
          It would be most offensive.

        You do me, lady, utmost grace,
        So I shall set out all my case,
          Displaying it before you,
        My coming here, its hows and whys,
        For I could never utter lies,
          Nor shall I, I assure you.

        I've loved you many and many a year,
        Although I've never journeyed here
          To show my love's anxiety.
        For when your master's here at home,
        A man can't chat with you alone –
          At least, not with propriety.

I heard one mention yesterday,
As I was musing on my way,
  Your man, your noble warder.
I heard the worthy man had gone
To market out at Botolfston
  On Lincoln's eastern border.

And since I knew that he was out,
That is why I've gone about
  To have this conversation.
Happy the man and gay his life
Who can dispose of such a wife
  In splendid isolation!

So come, dear lady, and agree,
And now and everlastingly
  I'll secretly adore you.

MARGERY: By Jesus Christ our heavenly king,
I swear that I'll do no such thing!
  May God above restore you!

I have my lord who is my spouse,
Who took me virgin to his house;
  In honour did we do it.
I love him well and he loves me;
Steel-true is our fidelity,
  And we shall never rue it.

Although he's working far away,
I should be wrong to go astray
  And set up as a whore.
Oh no! I never shall contract
To do that very faithless act
  In bed or on the floor.[1]

1. In the tragic love ballad, 'Glasgerion', in which a servant (significantly named Jack, like the jolly lover in poem no. 58) impersonates his prince on a night love visit to the King of Normandy's daughter, the lady's suspicion that he is not her royal lover begins when he possesses her churlishly on the floor instead of in the bed. Margery's imagination is too precise.

My man I never would beguile,
Though he were many a hundred mile
   Beyond celestial Rome.
No lure on earth, however great
Would make me take a man as mate
   Before my lord come home.

WILLIKIN: Lady, lady, change your mind!
You once were courteous, once were kind,
   And shall be so again.
Do it for God, who made us both!
Please think afresh, and don't be loath:
   Have pity on my pain!

MARGERY: Alas! alas! Am I a fool?
I swear, if I may thrive till Yule,
   You've had a stupid dream.
Me think afresh! Nothing so base!
My lord's a man of might and grace,
   And held in much esteem.

And I'm a wife both good and true;
A truer one man never knew
   In all our generation.
That man shall always be denied
Who woos me with his sensual pride
   To harm my reputation.

WILLIKIN: Sweetheart darling, mercy, please!
Such open villainies as these
   Are not what I propose.
As one in search of loving favour,
I ask a love of secret savour,
   The more the better, God knows.

MARGERY: I swear I'll never feed again
If you've not wasted all your pain;
So off you go, beloved brother!
I won't have you, nor any other
Except my husband. Go away,
For that's what I shall always say.

WILLIKIN: Yes, my lady: so I suppose.
So that poor man is sunk in woes
Who sweats and toils without success.
He can but grieve, I must confess.

And as for me, I'll say just this:
Yours is the love that I shall miss.

So madam, may I say good day?
And Christ who holds eternal sway
So work it that you change your view,
And I no longer mourn for you.

MINSTREL: So, feeling glum, he went away,
And racked his brain by night and day
   To find a way to change her.
A friend said: 'Now then, don't despair!
See Dame Siriz: in an affair
   She's not a bad arranger.'

So off he went without delay,
And shut his eyes upon the way,
   Thus dodging every meeting.
Though bursting with his grief and rage,
His words to her were mild and sage:
   He gave her gentle greeting.

WILLIKIN: Ah, Dame Siriz! And may God bless you!
I come in order to address you
   On the subject of my need;
And if you give me sustenation,
You shall have, as compensation,
   A rich reward indeed.

DAME SIRIZ: You're very welcome, lovely youth!
And if I can assist, in truth
I'll up and do my very best.
So let me listen to your request.

WILLIKIN: Ah, dear old lady, grim despair
Is blasting me with woe and care!

Mighty misery mars my life,
And all because of one sweet wife;
   And Margery is her name.
For I have loved her many a day,
And yet she firmly says me nay. –
   That is why I came.

And if her feelings are not changed,
For grief I shall become deranged,
  Or end my wretched life.
Yes, I thought of suicide
Until a friend made me decide
  To tell you all, old wife.

He told me that, beyond all doubt,
You could bring my aims about
  And rescue me from woe
By certain crafts and things you do.
You'll find great riches will accrue
  If you can work it so.

DAME SIRIZ: Benedicite be herein!
Dear boy, this is the way to sin.
Oh Lord! Oh Lord! for His sweet name,
May it not count to you for shame!
God's anger you will surely stir
If you put on me this slur.
For I am old and sick and lame;
Disease has made me meek and tame.
Bless you! Bless you, dear young chap,
In case you suffer some mishap
For slandering me with your suspicion –
And me in such a frail condition!
I am a dame of godly parts
And have no skill in magic arts.
A virtuous daily life I lead
With Paternoster and with Creed,
Which help good people in their need.
These grant us all success in life,
Including me, a poor old wife.
Confound the man who sent you here,
And may his soul be struck with fear!
May God in justice spoil his luck
For saying I would have such truck!

WILLIKIN: Dear lady, trust me when I say,
Quite other sense my words convey.
The man who sent me merely stated
You'd see our quarrel was abated.
So if you make a sweet accord
Between myself and my adored,

I'll give you gifts in plenteous store,
Many a mark and pounds galore,
Warm slippers and a fur-lined dress —
If your efforts have success.
And if you help your uttermost,
Many benefits might you boast.

DAME SIRIZ: Now Willikin, don't lie to me.
In truth, d'you speak this seriously?
D'you love the Lady Margery?

WILLIKIN: Yes, old lady, passionately.
I love her madly, fit to kill,
Unless I bend her to my will.

DAME SIRIZ: I pity you, dear Willikin:
May God ensure you quickly win!

Now if I knew you'd keep it dark,
I think I safely might embark
    On seeking what you covet.
So raise your hand and swear to bind
Yourself to silence: then I'll find
    A way to tell her of it.

I would not for the world be brought
Before the Bishop's holy court
    For playing such a game.
Their judgement would be quickly given,
And I upon an ass be driven
    By priests in utter shame.

WILLIKIN: But, mother, I in truth should hate
Disgrace and shame to be your fate
    Through striving for my good.
I shall fight with all my might
To keep it secret: here I plight
    My faith, by Holy Rood!

DAME SIRIZ: Welcome words, my Willikin!
And now it's settled, I'll begin
    A plan you'll find contenting.
In time to come you'll bless this day;
So perk up, man! Be blithe and gay,
    And stop all that lamenting.

You came here on your lucky day!
I'll visit her without delay,
   And give her cause to ponder.
On your behalf I'll so contrive
There won't be any man alive
   Of whom she will be fonder.

WILLIKIN: Well spoken, Dame Siriz! I vow
The peace of God is with me now,
   And luck shall come to you.
Now take this pound, and with it **buy**
Sheep for fold and pig for sty,
   As earnest of your due.

DAME SIRIZ: I swear by the joys of floor and roof
No pound was spent in any behoof
   Of half such power as this is!
For you shall see a wonder done,
The craftiest trick beneath the sun!
   Come, pup! Obey your missus!

Here's some pepper you must eat,
And mustard in the place of meat,
   To wet your little eye.
When the tears begin to dribble,
I shall invent a cunning quibble –
   And I know where and why.

WILLIKIN: What is the good of such a game?
I swear you've lost your wits, old dame.
Feeding mustard to a bitch!

DAME SIRIZ: Be quiet, fool! Control your itch!
For with this trick, by God above,
I'll make her give you all her love.
Nor shall I have a minute's rest
Until I've seen our efforts blessed.
Wait here for me till I come home!

WILLIKIN: Yes, by all the summer bloom,
Nothing shall drag me from your door
Until you come back here once more.

MINSTREL: So Dame Siriz began to go,
Pretending to be sunk in woe,
    Towards the lady's dwelling;
And, at the portal bowing low,
She made a mighty mournful show,
    Thus her fable telling:

DAME SIRIZ: Oh Lord! Oh Lord! the fate of wives!
Poor and wretched all their lives!
No man can suffer like a wife
Left without the means of life!
And that's my case, you will admit,
For I can neither walk nor sit.
I'm almost parched and starved to death;
I wish I hadn't another breath.
With cold and hunger I'm so whacked
My limbs won't work, and that's a fact.
Will no good person kindly fetch
Away the soul of such a wretch?

MARGERY: Good woman, may the Lord unbind you!
At once, this very day, I'll find you
    Meat, for love of God.
I greatly pity your distress,
For you have got a shabby dress,
    And you are badly shod.

Come in at once and have some food.

DAME SIRIZ: May God reward you for doing good!
And He who hung upon the Rood,
Who fasted forty days, and who
Rules earth and heaven, reward you too!

MARGERY: Here's bread and meat: sit down and dine!
And here's a cup brimful of wine.
Make merry! Please do what I ask,
And God reward you for your task!

MINSTREL: Then said that ancient crafty dame
(And Christ should really curse her name):

DAME SIRIZ: All sins I would forgive
The man who would cut off my head.
Oh, how I wish that I were dead!
But still – alas! – I live.

MARGERY: Good dame, of what do you complain?

DAME SIRIZ: The reason for my woe is plain.
    I had a daughter fair.
You never saw a lovelier face:
Her husband, too, was full of grace,
    Noble beyond compare.

My daughter loved him past belief,
And that is why I moan with grief.
Her husband left the house one day –
He had some business far away –
And that – alas! was what undid her.
A tonsured cleric came and bid her,
With cunning words and haughty glances,
To be his lover. These advances
The girl refused: and he could say
Nothing to help him get his way.

But then he started to bewitch,
And changed my daughter to a bitch.
And this is she of whom I tell:
My heart was broken by that spell.
Look how her eyes are simply streaming,
And on her cheeks the tears are gleaming.
You see, dear lady, it's no wonder
My wretched heart has burst asunder.
So any young and pretty wife
Shows how little she loves her life
If when a cleric plays the squire
She doesn't yield to his desire.

MARGERY: Beloved Christ! The other day
A cleric came in such a way
    And I refused his love.
I'm sure that he will change my shape!
Old lady, how shall I escape?
    Help me, by God above!

DAME SIRIZ: Already God has given you help,
Because you're not a bitch or whelp.
But if another clerk should come,
Dear girl, you must at once succumb.
Do as he says, that's my advice,
And be his love at any price.
If you say 'No' to his demand,
You'll surely get a worse command.

MARGERY: Beloved Christ! Oh, wretched day!
That cleric sadly went away
   Before he'd even won me.
Beyond all love of goods or fee,
I wish that once he'd lain with me –
   And then again had done me.

I'll love you, granddam, evermore
If you bring Willikin to my door,
   The cleric of whom I tell.
I'll give you gifts and prosper you
By anything that I can do,
   I swear it by God's bell.

DAME SIRIZ: In very truth, my dear young dame,
If I may search, and get no blame,
   I'll seek the fellow out.
If in the street or by the gate
I see him, I shan't hesitate
   To speak, you needn't doubt.

Good day, my lady! Off I go.

MARGERY: And as I have instructed, so
   You'll do it, won't you, dear?
I'll never laugh again or sing
Or be content, unless you bring
   Willikin to me here.

DAME SIRIZ: My dear young lady, if I may,
I'll bring the gentleman here today,
   Or use my best endeavour.

MINSTREL: So home she went and, going in,
There she found our Willikin,
   As tense, by God, as ever.

DAME SIRIZ: Sweet Willikin! No more distress,
For in your errand I've had success!
   She sent me out to get you.
So quickly up and follow, sir!
The thing you want to do to her,
   She promised me she'd let you.

WILLIKIN: May God who rules both earth and heaven
            Reward you, mother, seven times seven!

MINSTREL: With Dame Siriz at once he went
            To see his mistress with intent,
                And there at the lady's dwelling
            Siriz explained how she had found
            Our Willikin; and oaths profound
                And holy graced the telling.

DAME SIRIZ: Young lady, I looked for Willikin,
            And now I've brought the good man in.

MARGERY: Welcome, Willikin, darling thing!
            You are more welcome than the King!

            Oh, Willikin, my precious sweeting,
            I give you my most loving greeting,
                And all your will beside.
            You see I've wholly changed my mind:
            I wouldn't dream of being unkind
                In case you drooped and died!

WILLIKIN: Lady, by my fasts till noon,
            I shall devotedly and soon
                Accomplish what you say.
            And now, old mother, you must go;
            For by my faith, you surely know
                That she and I must play.

DAME SIRIZ: God knows I'll leave you, holy sir!
            And see you dibble deep in her
                And stretch her thighs out wide.
            God visit you with every pest
            If you give her any rest
                Whilst lying there inside!

(ad omnes)   And so, if any man lacks sense,
            And can't, in spite of all expense,
                Bring his darling to it,
            I'm ready, if he'll only pay
            To set him on the winning way,
                For I know how to do it!

96

THE FOX AND THE WOLF IN THE WELL

A famished Fox in gloomy mood
Left the wood in search of food.
Such fearful pangs he'd never had,
Nor felt a hunger half as bad.
He kept away from path and street,
For men he did not wish to meet.
He'd rather meet a single hen
Than half a hundred women then.
Advancing swiftly over all,
He saw, not far away, a wall
Around a house; and now he yearned
To ease the pangs which in him burned.
So starved he was, he couldn't think
Of anything but food and drink.
Eagerly he looked around
And then rushed out across the ground
Towards the wall which, when he neared,
Partly broken down appeared,
Yes, just as if it had been knocked,
Although the gate beside was locked.
The nearest opening that he found,
He leaped and twitched through at a bound,
And then he gave a scornful grin –
Funny to think that he was in
Without so much as by-your-leave
To warden of the hedge or reeve![1]
   A shed was there, with open door,
Through which some hens had crept before,
Five in fact, which makes a flock,
And sitting with them was a Cock.
{ Before the hens could do a thing,
{ Fox had spoilt their gathering:
{ He nipped the necks of the fattest three
{ And started eating cheerfully.[2]
The two survivors of the flock
Had flown aloft; and so had Cock.

1. The hedge-warden was employed to guard crops in closed fields.

2. These four lines have been inserted to cover what appears to be an omission in the text.

'What are you up to here?' said Cock,
'Christ give you grief! Go home, old Fox!
You often do our henfolk shame.'
'Be quiet, I beg you, in God's name!'
Fox replied. 'Sir Chanticleer!
Fly you down and come you near.
I've nothing done down here but good:
I've let your hens a little blood;
Believe me, they were pretty sick;
They wouldn't have lived another week
Without that opening of their veins.
This work I did for henfolk's gains
And charity's sake. I let their blood:
The same, Sir Cock, would do you good.
Your spleen, like theirs, is over-hot.
Not ten days more on nest you'll squat;
Your life will finish in a trice
Unless you take my sage advice.
I'll let your blood beneath the breast,
Or call the priest – he'll do the rest!'
'Away!' cried Cock. 'And droop in pain,
For you have been my people's bane.
Go, with nothing as reward,
And may you be by God abhorred!
For were I down, by God's own name,
I could be sure of further shame.
But if it chanced to reach the ear
Of our cellarer that you were here,
He'd come pursuing you at once
With hefty pikes and staves and stones.
All your bones he'd break in two,
And then we'd be revenged on you.'

    Fox stayed quiet, and said no more.
His thirst was raging mighty sore;
In fact, it pained him rather worse
Than his hunger had at first.
He started hunting all around
And soon his ranging senses found
A craftily constructed well,
With water in, as he could tell.
Two hanging buckets there he found;
One, at the bottom, touched the ground,

And when its rope was upwards wound,
This bucket upped, the other downed.
How it worked he couldn't decide:
He seized the bucket, leapt inside
In expectation of a drink,
And then the bucket began to sink.
Too late! For Fox had not foreseen
He'd be a part of the machine.
He pondered the device in pain,
But all his ponderings were vain.
Bamboozled as he was by it,
He must continue down the pit.
Far better had it been his will
To leave the bucket hanging still!
And what with misery and with dread,
All thoughts of thirst clean left his head.
In such a mood he came to ground;
Abundant water there he found,
But as the liquid seemed to stink,
He didn't stoop and have a drink,
Because his mind was off his thirst.
Then Fox exclaimed, 'May greed be curst!
It makes a fellow overfeed.
Now if I hadn't had this greed,
I shouldn't have landed in this woe
Through belly-pleasure, that I know.
Grief to the man in any land
Who pilfers with a thieving hand!
I'm neatly trapped, it's pretty clear,
Or else some devil brought me here.
I used to be a clever chap,
But now I'm in another's trap.'

Most piteously Fox then wept.
Now quickly from the forest depth
A Wolf came out in search of food,
Running in a famished mood.
Although he'd searched the livelong night,
He hadn't had a single bite.
Close by the wall, he heard a noise,
And recognized his neighbour's voice;
He knew this Fox, who always stood
As godsire to his own young brood.

So by the well he stopped and sat,
And then called out, 'Now what is that
I hear below me in the well?
Are you a Christian, or my pal?
Be truthful now, don't falsify:
Who put you down the well, and why?'
Now Fox knew well who had arrived,
And thinking fast, at once contrived
A trick by which he'd upwards go
Himself, and send the wolf below.
So he called out, 'Now who's up there?
I think it's Sigrim that I hear.'[1]
Then answered Wolf, 'That's very true,
But who, God counsel you, are you?'
'I'll tell you,' was the sly reply,
'And not one word'll be a lie.
My name is Reynard: I'm your friend,
And if I'd thought that you'd descend,
Old man, I would have sent for you
To come with me – and that is true.'
'With you?' was Wolf's reply. 'Where to?
Down in the well, what should I do?'
So Fox explained, 'You are not wise,
For here's the bliss of paradise,
Where miseries and troubles never
Come and I may thrive for ever.
Food there is, and drink there is;
No need to work to get your bliss.
Hunger can't exist down here,
And other sorrows don't appear.
There's plenty here of all things good.'
    This raised in Wolf a festive mood.
'God counsel you, but are you dead,
Or of this world?' Wolf gaily said.
'When did you die, and why and how,
And what are you up to down there now?
It's hardly three days since that we –
Yourself, your wife, your family
Of children large and small, and I –
Sat down to eat in company.'

1. Traditional name for the wolf, as Reynard was for the fox.

Fox answered him, 'Yes, that is so.
And, God be thanked, as matters go,
I've come to Jesus here below;
But none of my acquaintance know.
I wouldn't be with them up there
For all the wealth on earth, I swear.
Why should a man in the world go,
Where nothing comes but grief and woe,
And filth and sin are all he finds?
But here are joys of many kinds.
Here are sheep and goats in plenty.'

    Now Wolf was literally empty,
Not having fed for hours on end.
'Aha!' he said. 'My dearest friend,
Allow me to come down and share
Whatever victuals you have there,
And I'll forget your many crimes
Of stealing food in former times.
For these you shall be well forgiven.'
'Oh yes,' said Fox, 'if you were shriven;
If sinful ways you would abjure,
And if your life were clean and pure,
Then I should gladly recommend
Permission for you to descend.'
'But,' Wolf exclaimed, 'to whom should I
Confess my sins? For here my eye
Sees not one man or thing alive
Equipped or qualified to shrive.
Will you, so often my friend sincere,
Listen to my confession here,
And all my life I'll tell to you.'
'That,' said Fox, 'you shall not do!'
Then Wolf entreated, 'By your grace,
For hunger weakens me apace!
Tonight I shall be dead unless
You solace me whilst I confess.
For the love of Christ, please be my priest!'

    Then he bowed, the mournful beast,
And loudly sighed. 'If you desire
Your shrift,' said Fox, 'then I require
That you shall tell me, one by one,
Your sins until the last is done.'
'Gladly', said Wolf, 'and straight away!

I have been wicked all my days.
Besides, I have the widows' curse,
And that makes all my sins look worse.
I've tasted quite a thousand sheep –
And thinking of it makes me weep –
In fact, that's less than the proper score.
Master, must I tell you more?'
'Yes,' said Fox, 'and nothing spare;
Or you must find a priest elsewhere.'
Then said Wolf, 'Dear friend and true,
Forgive my saying ill of you!
Men said that in your time of life
You did transgression with my wife.
I once observed you at it with her,
On finding you in bed together.
Indeed, you often caught my eye,
Being bedded down, and me nearby.
So I believe, as others do,
That what I saw was wholly true.
And so I hated you, no doubt.
Dear friend, I beg, don't be put out.'
    'Wolf,' then Fox declared to him,
'Every single sort of sin
That you have done in thought, speech, deed,
I now forgive you in your need.'
'May Christ reward your saying so!'
Said Wolf, now free of every woe.
'Now I've purified my life,
I do not think of child or wife.
Tell me quick, what must I do
In order to descend to you?'
'Do?' said Fox. 'I'll make that clear.
You see a bucket hanging near?
That's the gate of heaven's bliss.
Jump in – take care that you don't miss! –
And you shall quickly come to me.'
'I shall', said Wolf, 'most easily!'
Then, as Fox had calculated,
In he leapt. The bucket, weighted,
Lowered Wolf, and lifted Fox.
The former, worried by the shock,
Cried out half-way in his descent
To Fox, as up the latter went,

'Dear friend, what shall I do, and how?
And tell me where you're going now.'
'Where?' said Fox. 'Why, up, my friend –
May God this course of mine commend!
And you go down and find your victual –
Loot, I fear, worth very little.
But one thing makes me glad, I'm sure:
You go down there confessed and pure.
I'll see to it your death-knell's rung,
And masses for your soul are sung.'
      Below, the wretch found only water.
His raging hunger gave no quarter.
He had a cold feast down below,
With only frogs to knead his dough!
Down the well the tricked Wolf stood,
Famished and in frenzied mood.
He cursed the one who'd brought him there,
Which didn't burden Fox with care.
      Now in a building nearby,
There lived some friars sleek and sly;
And when it was the time of day
For all these friars to rise and pray,
They had a man whose duty lay
In waking them without delay,
And then their matins they could say.
He said, 'Get up, each mother's son,
And come to matins, everyone!'
This friar's name was Aylmer:
He was the master gardener,
And, feeling thirsty during prayers,
He left those heavenly affairs,
And went towards the well at speed
To satisfy his simple need.
Once there, he pulled with vigour great,
But he found Wolf a heavy weight.
He hauled and pulled with all his might
Until the beast came into sight,
When, seeing him sitting there inside,
'The Devil's in the well!' he cried.
Then out the friars dashed, pell-mell,
And hurried quickly to the well.
Pikes and staves and stones they had,
And those unarmed felt very sad.

They hoisted Wolf from down the well.
He had too many foemen fell,
Keen to have him slit by hounds,
And beaten and given gaping wounds!
With thwacking staves and stinging spears,
They battered Wolf about the ears.
Fox had tricked him, I declare;
He didn't find much bliss down there,
Nor get forgiveness, heaven knows,
For undergoing all those blows!

PROVENANCE OF THE POEMS

KEY

D & W : *Early Middle English Texts* (Dickins and Wilson), Bowes & Bowes 1951

CB13 : *English Lyrics of the Thirteenth Century* (Carleton Brown), O.U.P. 1932

CB14 : *Religious Lyrics of the Fourteenth Century* (Carleton Brown), O.U.P. 1952

Rob. : *Secular Lyrics of the Fourteenth and Fifteenth Centuries* (R. H. Robbins), O.U.P. 1956

Sis. : *Fourteenth Century Verse and Prose* (Kenneth Sisam), O.U.P. 1921

Min. : *Poems of Laurence Minot* (Hall 3rd edition), O.U.P. 1914

C & S : *Early English Lyrics* (Chambers and Sidgwick), Sidgwick Jackson 1949

Gre. : *The Early English Carols* (Richard L. Greene), O.U.P. 1935

Ed. McKnight : *Middle English humorous Tales in Verse*, Boston 1913

Hall : *Selections from Early Middle English*, O.U.P. 1920

Fur. : *Political, Religious and Love Poems* (F. J. Furnivall), O.U.P. (Early English Text Society) 1866

Bro. : *The Harley Lyrics* (G. L. Brook), Manchester University Press 1956

Poem No.	Source	Page	Poem No.	Source	Page	Poem No.	Source	Page
1	C & S	177	15	CB14	2	29	CB13	15
2	CB13	55	16	Gre.	119	30	Fur.	239
3	CB13	22	17	CB14	17	31	Fur.	242
4	CB13	24	18	CB14	65	32	CB13	85
5	C & S	103	19	CB13	3	33	CB13	1
6	Fur.	226	20	CB13	27	34	CB13	33
7	Gre.	9	21	CB13	68	35	Fur.	224
8	CB14	78	22	C & S	102	36	CB13	126
9	CB13	38	23	Sis.	37	37	CB14	3
10	CB13	1	24	CB13	14	38	CB13	101
11	Fur.	214	25	C & S	170	39	C & S	187
12	Gre.	193	26	CB13	54	40	C & S	186
13	CB13	61	27	CB13	31	41	C & S	183
14	CB14	3	28	CB13	130	42	C & S	192

Poem No.	Source	Page	Poem No.	Source	Page	Poem No.	Source	Page
43	Fur.	96	62	Bro.	69	80	Bro.	56
44	Hall	176	63	CB13	133	81	Bro.	54
45	Hall	183	64	Fur.	237	82	Bro.	70
46	D&W	60	65	Fur.	237	83	Bro.	71
47	Rob.	11	66	Fur.	237	84	Bro.	43
48	Rob.	12	67	CB13	131	85	Bro.	33
49	Rob.	12	68	Min.	4	86	Bro.	37
50	Rob.	12	69	Sis.	157	87	Bro.	40
51	Rob.	233	70	Ed. Bateson		88	Bro.	31
52	CB13	32		Ed. Gordon		89	Bro.	34
53	Sis.	163	71	Ed. Gollancz		90	Bro.	44
54	CB13	107	72	Bro.	29	91	Bro.	63
55	Rob.	15	73	Bro.	46	92	Bro.	39
56	Rob.	40	74	Bro.	35	93	Bro.	62
57	Rob.	41	75	Bro.	68	94	Sis.	14
58	Rob.	24	76	Bro.	53	95	Ed. McKnight	
59	Rob.	18	77	Bro.	60	96	Ed. McKnight	
60	Rob.	105	78	Bro.	57			
61	Rob.	106	79	Bro.	59			

APPENDIX II

FURTHER BIBLIOGRAPHY

LITERARY AND CRITICAL

Atkins, J. W. H., *English Literary Criticism, the Medieval Phase*, C.U.P. 1943

Bayley, John, *The Characters of Love*, Constable 1961

Bennett, H. S., *Chaucer and the Fifteenth Century*, O.U.P. 1947

Bowra, Sir C. M., *Medieval Love-Song* (John Coffin Memorial Lecture), U.L.P. 1961

Cawley, A. C. (ed.), *Everyman and Medieval Miracle Plays*, Dent 1956

Chambers, E. K., *The Medieval Stage*, O.U.P. 1903

Chambers, E. K., *English Literature at the Close of the Middle Ages*, O.U.P. 1945

Chaucer, Geoffrey, *Poetical Works*, ed. F. N. Robinson, Houghton Mifflin 1933

Craig, Hardin, *English Religious Drama of the Middle Ages*, O.U.P. 1955

Davies, R. T., *Medieval English Lyrics*, Faber 1963

Everett, Dorothy, *Essays on ME Literature* (ed. Patricia Kean), O.U.P. 1955

Gower, *Complete Works*, ed. G. C. Macaulay, 1889–1902

Ker, W. P., *Medieval English Literature*, O.U.P. 1912

Langland, *Vision of Pierce Plowman*, ed. W. W. Skeat, Early English Text Society 1869

Lewis, C. S., *The Allegory of Love*, O.U.P. 1935

Loomis, G. R., *The Development of Arthurian Romance*, Hutchinson 1963

Mandeville, Sir John, *Travels*, ed. Malcolm Letts, Hakluyt Society. 1954

Owst, G. R., *Literature and Pulpit in Medieval England*, C.U.P. 1933

Spiers, John, *Medieval English Poetry*, Faber 1957

Waddell, Helen, *The Wandering Scholars*, Penguin 1954

Waddell, Helen, *Medieval Latin Lyrics*, Penguin 1952

Waddell, Helen, *Peter Abelard; a novel*, Collins 1958

Weston, Jessie L., *From Ritual to Romance*, Macmillan 1920

Wickham, Glynne, *Early English Stages*, Vol. 1., Routledge 1959

Williamson, Hugh Ross, *The Arrow and the Sword* (2nd ed.), Faber 1955

Wilson, R. M., *Early ME. Literature*, Methuen 1951

Wilson, R. M., *The Lost Literature of Medieval England*, Methuen 1952

Young, Karl, *The Drama of the Medieval Church*, O.U.P. 1933

HISTORICAL

Anderson, M. D., *Misericords; Medieval Life in English Woodcarving*, Penguin 1954

Bett, Henry, *English Myths and Traditions*, Batsford 1952

Brooke, Iris, *English Costume of the Early Middle Ages*, Black 1936

Brooke, Iris, *English Costume of the Later Middle Ages*, Black 1935

Cave, C. J. P., *Roof Bosses in Medieval Churches*, Cambridge 1948

Cave, C. J. P., *Medieval Carvings in Exeter Cathedral*, Penguin 1953

Clark, Sir K., *The Nude*, Murray 1956

Coulton, G. G., *Medieval Panorama*, Macmillan 1944

Culpeper, *Complete Herbal*, Joseph 1947

Gardner, Arthur, *Minor English Wood Sculpture 1400–1550*, Tiranti 1959

Hassall, W. O., *How They Lived* (55 B.C.–A.D. 1485), Blackwell 1957

Heer, Friedrich, *The Medieval World*, Weidenfeld & Nicolson 1961

Houston, Mary G., *Medieval Costume in England and France*, Black 1939

Kunz, George F., *The Curious Lore of Precious Stones*, Lippincott, 1913

Norris, Herbert, *Costume and Fashion* (Vol. 2, Senlac to Bosworth), Dent 1927

Pevsner, Nikolaus, *The Leaves of Southwell*, Penguin 1945

Power, Eileen, *Medieval People*, Methuen 1924

Stone, Lawrence, *Sculpture in Britain: The Middle Ages*, Penguin 1955

Streeter, Edwin W., *Precious Stones and Gems*, Bell 1898.

Trevelyan, G. M., *English Social History*, Longmans 1944

Victoria and Albert Museum, *Gospel Stories in English Embroidery*, H.M.S.O. 1964

REFERENCE

Brewer, Rev. E. Cobham, *A Dictionary of Phrase and Fable*, Cassell, undated

Cambridge History of English Literature, Vols. I and II.

The Catholic Encyclopaedia

Dictionary of National Biography

The Jewish Encyclopaedia

Legouis and Cazamian, *A History of English Literature*, Dent 1957

Shipley, J. T., *Dictionary of World Literary Terms*, Allen & Unwin 1955

Stratmann, F. H., *Middle English Dictionary* (ed. H. Bradley) O.U.P., 1891

Standard Dictionary of Folklore, Mythology and Legend, Funk & Wagnalls 1950